To my parents

Long Black Song

The University Press of Virginia
Copyright © 1972 by the Rector and Visitors
of the University of Virginia

Second printing 1973

ISBN: 0–8139–0403–x
Library of Congress Catalog Card Number: 72–77261
Printed in the United States of America

The author wishes to express his gratitude for permission to
reprint the following:
H. Rap Brown, from *Die Nigger Die!*, copyright © 1969 by
Lynne Brown; reprinted by permission of the publisher, The
Dial Press. Paul Laurence Dunbar, "An Ante-Bellum Sermon" from *The Collected Poems of Paul Laurence Dunbar*;
reprinted by permission of Dodd, Mead and Co. Robert
Hayden, "Runagate Runagate," from *Selected Poems*, copyright © 1966 by Robert Hayden; reprinted by permission of
October House Inc. James Weldon Johnson, "Listen Lord—
A Prayer," from *God's Trombones* by James Weldon John-
son, copyright 1927 by the Viking Press, Inc., renewed 1955
by Grace Nail Johnson; reprinted by permission of the Viking Press, Inc. Claude McKay, sestet from "The Negro's
Tragedy," from *Selected Poems of Claude McKay*, copyright
1953 by Bookman Associates; reprinted by permission of
Twayne Publishers, Inc. Dudley Randall, "Booker T. and
W. E. B."; reprinted by permission of the author. A revised
version of "Completely Well: One View of Black American
Culture" is reprinted by permission of the publisher from
Key Issues in the Afro-American Experience, Volume I,
edited by Nathan I. Huggins, et al., © 1971 by Harcourt
Brace Jovanovich, Inc. The Bibliography is reprinted from
Black Literature in America, edited by Houston A. Baker,
Jr., by permission of McGraw-Hill Book Co.

Long Black Song

Essays in Black American Literature

and Culture

Houston A. Baker, Jr.

The University Press of Virginia

Charlottesville

. . . what I write is urged out of my blood.
There is no white man who could write my book,
Though many think their story should be told
Of what the Negro people ought to brook.
Our statesmen roam the world to set things right.
This Negro laughs and prays to God for Light!

Claude McKay

Acknowledgments

When a book is completed, it is pleasant to think back on those whose concern and assistance helped make it possible. I am especially grateful to Arna Bontemps for his encouragement and continuing interest. Ernest Kaiser was a constant help, and the staff of the Schomburg Library showed me every kindness. I would also like to thank Miss Frances Lackey, my typist; James Nash of the University Press of Virginia; Professors David Levin of the University of Virginia and Richard Sylvester of Yale University for their confidence and support. Above all, I am grateful to my wife Charlotte and my son Mark, who endured.

H.A.B.

University of Virginia
February, 1972

Contents

I. Completely Well: One View of
Black American Culture　　　　　　　　　　1

II. Black Folklore and the Black American
Literary Tradition　　　　　　　　　　18

III. Freedom and Apocalypse: A Thematic
Approach to Black Expression　　　　　　42

IV. Revolution and Reform: Walker, Douglass,
and the Road to Freedom　　　　　　　58

V. Men and Institutions: Booker T. Washington's
Up from Slavery　　　　　　　　　　84

VI. The Black Man of Culture: W. E. B. Du Bois
and *The Souls of Black Folk*　　　　　　96

VII. From the Improbable Fields Down South:
One View of Ghetto Language and Culture　　109

VIII. Racial Wisdom and Richard Wright's *Native Son*　　122

IX. Conclusion　　　　　　　　　　142

Bibliography　　　　　　　　　　147

Index　　　　　　　　　　153

Long Black Song

I Completely Well

One View of Black American Culture

The Question of "Culture"

MOST of modern Western civilization uses the word *culture* to mean only "a body of intellectual and imaginative work"[1] and considers it something spiritual and transcendent. In general, those who have this reverential attitude toward culture also have the greatest vested interest in preserving its present limited connotations. Hopefully, through sound reasoning and serious effort the true meaning of the word can be reestablished. Culture is not transcendental and ethereal; while some of its manifestations—some of its arts and artifacts—may often be defined in spiritual terms, culture itself is a more inclusive concept that accurately denotes "a whole way of life." To define or analyze a culture, therefore, one must pay as much attention to historical factors as one pays to technology and to sociological patterns. The proposition here is that the history of a culture is, in effect, the culture. Culture is not a body of intellectual and imaginative work that can be set forth as a sanctuary from our technological age; it is not a series of artifacts displayed by curators of museums; it is not the curriculum of even the most advanced and highly esteemed university; and it most certainly is not the supernatural ethos that surrounds these things. One does not worship, display, or teach culture; one acknowledges it as a whole way of life grounded in the past, and one necessarily lives a culture.

The central question of the discussion that follows is whether a way of life known as black American culture is distinct and separate from a way of life known as white culture. The relevance of historical information in arriving at an answer cannot be overrated. If, as proposed here, the history of a people is the

---

[1] Raymond Williams, *Culture and Society, 1780–1950* (New York, 1958), p. 325.

culture, then the history of the black American is black American
culture, and the only way to arrive at an understanding of black
American culture is to comprehend fully the history of the black
American. Moreover, to survey the evolution of his way of life
is to analyze why *culture* came to be defined in America as something spiritual, transcendental, and white. For some, the most
vexing problem surrounding such an examination is the fear that
black American culture may prove separate and unequal. However, "separate and unequal" in the question of culture is as much
a myth as "separate but equal" in the question of school facilities.
Any whole way of life differs from any other whole way of life
in content and form, but discussions of the relative value of different cultures can only lead to distortions and faulty evaluations.
The attempt here, then, is not to demonstrate the equality of
black American culture but to deal with its distinctiveness from
another whole way of life. We must begin with history, the primary factor in such a discussion, and move on to study the distortions occasioned by race and culture theorizing, the literary
reflections of a black culture, and, finally, the wholesome effects
of acknowledging a distinct black American culture.

The History

Any black American might paraphrase Countee Cullen and
ask: "What is America to me? / Spacious sky / And land of liberty?" The answer history supports is that America is something
apart. Black Americans were driven through the amber waves of
grain, their stars and stripes the engravings of cat-o'-nine-tails on
black flesh. The legends of men conquering wild and virgin
lands are not the legends of black America; the stories of benevo-
lent theocracies bringing light and salvation to pagans are not
the stories of black America; and the tales of pioneers enduring
the hardships of the West for the promise of immense wealth are
not the tales of black America. When the black American reads
Frederick Jackson Turner's *The Frontier in American History*,
he feels no regret over the end of the Western frontier. To black
America, *frontier* is an alien word; for, in essence, all frontiers
established by the white psyche have been closed to the black
man.

In a recent work, Dr. James Comer deals with America's conception of frontiers. He points out that the early wealth of America was contingent upon the produce of its great land area and upon the ships that carried that produce to foreign ports; together, agriculture and shipping insured the survival of the country in its early days, and the wealth acquired from the partnership filled white coffers. Each proclamation of a new frontier brought substantially increased wealth to these two enterprises.

Both agriculture and shipping, however, were closed to the black American; when the American grab bag was opening—when new territories were being annexed and handed out to humble homesteaders—the black American was toiling from day clean to first dark. The railroads received phenomenal doles; miners claimed hundreds of acres; immigrants made their way into the Northwest Territory and established thriving communities. Meanwhile, the black American was sold or bartered back and forth as chattel. Only when the frontier had closed, only when the strings of the grab bag were pulling tight, did the black American begin to make his presence felt in a society that had not included him on its list of recipients. As Comer puts it: "Much of the wealth of America was given away while blacks were still in slavery. Almost all of it was given away before 1915 when 90 percent of the black population lived in extreme poverty and oppression in the Deep South."[2]

Yet, there are mythmakers who insist on reassuring the black man that whites came to North America with pennies and parlayed them into fortunes. They talk of the competitive spirit, justice for all, and bootstrap philosophies of advancement. This is simply naiveté. Even now they do not realize that the dreams, tales, and manners of black America are things apart from this American *Weltanschauung*; they do not realize that with every law and grant America took calculated steps to set the black man outside the larger society. While the mythmakers gaze back at what Baldwin has called a period of "European innocence," while they hear drums beating out the Spirit of Seventy-six, the black American looks back to Elmina on the Gold Coast and hears the debate on behalf of the three clauses in the Constitution that in-

2 James Comer, *Beyond Black and White* (New York, 1972).

sured the continuance of American slavery—the fugitive slave
clause, the slave trade clause, and the three-fifths clause.[3] Slavery
was written into the American Constitution, and, when its use-
fulness had begun to wane, the effects of the cotton gin revived it.
The perspectives of black America and white America are as far
apart as the captain's cabin and the holds full of "black ivory"
during the middle passage (the eight-week voyage from Africa
to the New World).

On one side the word is:

> If you see my Pompey, 30 yrs of age,
> new breeches, plain stockings, negro shoes;
> if you see my Anna, likely young mulatto
> branded E on the right cheek, R on the left,
> catch them if you can and notify subscriber.

On the other side the word is: "Mean mean mean to be free."
The polarity is so great that it is perhaps meaningless to debate
what was left of an African heritage after a "voyage through
death / to life upon these shores."[4] Melville J. Herskovits[5] argues
that much was left after the middle passage—African linguistic
traits, religious practices, patterns of family organization, and
modes of song and dance. However, E. Franklin Frazier tells us
that "the Negroes were practically stripped of their social heritage
and their traditional social organization was destroyed as the
result of the manner in which they were enslaved and became
the labour force in the plantation economy."[6] After Herskovits,
Frazier, and others have spoken, the fact remains that the black
American's perspective on history, his patterns of social organization, his life style as a whole, are significantly different from
those of white America. Some have attributed the differences to
race, others to culture. Heretofore, few have been willing to look
steadily at America's past and acknowledge that the differences
stem largely from the fact that the black man was denied his part
in the frontier and his share of the nation's wealth.

---

[3] See Benjamin Quarles, *The Negro in the Making of America* (New York, 1968),
p. 60.

[4] The preceding lines of poetry are from Robert Hayden, "Runagate Runagate,"
in *Selected Poems* (New York, 1966), pp. 75–77.

[5] Melville J. Herskovits, *The Myth of the Negro Past* (New York, 1941).

[6] E. Franklin Frazier, *The Negro Church in America* (New York, 1964), p. 82.

Race and Culture Theorizing

If one is to come to terms with the history, one must face the
fact that no meaningful definition of *race* exists. All arguments
to the contrary, *race* is simply a heuristic term that is often in-
voked in support of an existing order or in an attempt to unify a
body of people for political purposes. The theories—from Gobi-
neau to Shockley—merely serve to perpetuate superstition.[7] The
practice of superstition consists in setting the generalization over
the fact, and that is what all race theorizers have done. According
to the race theorizers, if one black man acts in a particular manner, all black men must act in the same manner. Similar skin
color, features, and hair type mean that all who possess them are
to be subsumed under a particular race theory. As Jacques Barzun has pointed out, such theorizing is not only insupportable
but also dangerous; it can lead only to blood baths.

The word *culture* is no more helpful than *race* without the
type of skilled analysis it has received at the hands of Raymond
Willams.[8] Used in a purely subjective or political context, it can
become simply a surrogate for *race*. In its contemporary sense,
culture is a product of the nineteenth century, which also fostered
the present institutional connotations of such words as *industry,
democracy, class,* and *art*. In response to the Industrial Revolution, certain moral and intellectual endeavors were designated
the components of "culture" and set apart from more functional
aspects of society. Thus, moral and intellectual activities were
set above processes of practical social judgment and became a
court of human appeal that sought an alternative to the times.
This designation of culture as a body of intellectual and imaginative work created a distilled version of the concept. In fact,
"culture" in its fullest sense was primarily a response to the industrial metamorphosis; many pre-industrial social endeavors
were not viable in an industrial society, and a new order had to
be established. The activities of this new order were segregated
under the heading of culture, and in this version it came to represent "a whole way of life." Therefore, until the full substance

7 Jacques Barzun, *Race: A Study in Superstition* (New York, 1937).
8 Williams, *Culture and Society*.

of the term—culture as a whole way of life—has been reasserted,
it cannot be used to discuss the differentiation between groups
of people without invoking the same superstition and meaningless appendages that accompany the word *race*.

Black America can justifiably say that it possesses a true culture—a *whole* way of life that includes its own standards of moral
and aesthetic achievement. The black American need not engage
in arguments over the superiority or the inferiority of particular
attributes; he need not fight pitched battles over different bodies
of intellectual and imaginative work and attempt to assess their
relative worth. A body of intellectual and imaginative work
reflects a whole way of life. And only that same culture can
evolve the standards by which its intellectual and imaginative
work is to be judged. The malaise of the black psyche has come,
in part, from the attempts of white America to set both "race"
and "culture" in an unreal context.

Not content with denying the black American the frontier
and a share of the nation's wealth, white America has attempted
to justify its denial. Race theories and the use of the word *culture*
in a slanted manner have allowed whites to state that black men
are part of an inferior race and possess no cultural capabilities.
The first assertion is sheer superstition; the second is grounded
on an attempt to use *culture* in a too limited context. By incul-
cation from generation to generation, however, white America
has succeeded in distorting the black psyche. This process is
obvious in the realm of race theorizing; the more subtle distortions occasioned by culture theorizing, however, can be illustrated by an autobiographical example.

Culture Theorizing and Its Distortions

"God's in his heaven / All's right with the world!" was one of
the first literary phrases from my mother's lips that fixed itself
in my mind. There were countless others. I specifically remember being overjoyed when I could match her word for word in
the first eighteen lines of the "General Prologue" to *The Canter-
bury Tales:* "Whan that Aprill with his shoures soote / The
droghte of March hath perced to the roote." I had heard her
quote the words time and again, but it was not until one hot

summer afternoon that I discovered they came from Chaucer. I was looking over the bookshelves upstairs; after a few minutes I pulled out *The Complete Works of Geoffrey Chaucer.* It was a moment of triumph when I was able to run downstairs and recite these lines for an admiring parent.

Looking back on that time, I remember the four or five long rows of shelves that held the family books: Rudyard Kipling, Robert Louis Stevenson, Charlotte Bonté, and a host of other white writers. I perused each of the books and looked forward to the day when I would be able to read them all with understanding.

In the meantime, there was the local "colored" library to satisfy my reading fancy. The black librarian was not a kindly old lady who steered me in the proper direction; she was quick-tempered and stern and handed over my officially charged-out volumes as though dispensing her personal property. And so every two weeks I walked or rode the bus to this august lady's library and checked out the allotted five books. I read the entire sports collection, which consisted of books about white athletes in white high schools, white colleges, or white major leagues. I read pioneering stories until the sound "Westward, ho!" rang in my ears twenty-four hours a day. All the pioneers, of course, were white; all the Indians, and even the beasts of the field, were "dark." I read biographies of American heroes and grew so inspired that I set up my own garage workshop in an attempt to emulate the performances of young Tom Edison and young Sam Morse. This was the world of the library until the great event occurred—the white library downtown was opened to "colored people"!

I walked between its grimy Ionian columns, across the shadows to the front door, and entered the lobby on tiptoe. There was an unbelievable bustle, strange after the small, cramped silences of the colored library. Here, there was light and activity, and an incredible sense of importance seemed to hang from the ceilings decorated with ancient, white figures. At the information desk, I finally attracted someone's attention and learned where the children's section was located. I tiptoed up the stairs and was greeted by a kindly white lady who smiled and asked if she could help me. "What sort of book do you want?" I told her I wanted sports stories, pioneer stories, or biographies, and she led me to the pioneer section. As she pulled out book after book, I watched this kind white lady turn redder and redder. I kept saying that I had read the books she pulled out, and she grew so incredulous that she finally submitted me to an oral examination on some innocuous story about a ten-year-old white boy who shot a mountain lion and saved his community. When I knew the answers, she slammed the book shut and simply pointed to where I could find the sports stories and the biographies. It did seem strange that the colored library and the white library had the *same* pioneer books.

Fortunately, I only had to use the children's section for a brief time. A whole new world opened to me with high school English and with the works of Plato, Voltaire, and Joyce that my brother brought home from college. When I finished high school there was little doubt in my mind that I wanted to study literature and get to know as much as possible about as many books as possible. However, the cultural bias reflected equally in the colored and white libraries was destined to recur in both a black college and a white graduate school. At the white graduate school, I read the *same* books that I had studied at the black college. When I asked at either school about the works of black writers, I was told that in English one need study only the "classical" works. A friend in graduate school attempted in vain to demonstrate that I should study black works since they were reflections of the whole way of life that I was living. Some time later, I did begin to deal with the works of black literature—when I was not pursuing the "classics."

My first job was teaching English—a course from Homer to Joyce. My colleagues, both old and young, knew little about black writers, and the syllabuses (like those in graduate school) were barren when it came to the names of black authors. Now, as I teach black American literature, I find few colleagues with whom I can really discuss the works that I am teaching; indeed, many of my associates think that black literature began with Richard Wright and ends with James Baldwin.

This pattern of events seems to offer a perfect example of culture theorizing and the distortions that it occasions. Born in a racialistic former slave state, I was bombarded with the words, images, and artifacts of the white world. My parents had been bombarded with the same images, and the black librarian was no better off. There are thousands of black men in America who have gone through similar experiences. Few of us realized that "the doctors" had bored holes in our heads, cut out part of our brains, and shot electricity through the rest.[9] All of us had been lobotomized into an acceptance of "culture" on the white world's terms; we failed to realize that the manner in which the white world used "culture" only helped justify its denial of the black man.

Having recovered or attempted to reconstruct that which was cut away, black Americans have now cast aside the etherizing veil; no longer can white America hide behind the culture curtain. Whites quote Matthew Arnold at blacks; they say that culture consists of the best that has been thought and known in the world. The world, of course, means the white world, and the best can only be that which is white and Western. To possess culture, according to whites, one has to possess a firm knowledge of the best that the white Western world has to offer, whether it is Beethoven or Brecht. That culture might stand for a whole way of life and that there might be a multitude of wholes never occurs to most white Americans. Those who have read Ruth Benedict or Margaret Mead do acknowledge that there are many cultures, but they seldom (if ever) admit that the "best" may lie somewhere beyond the narrow bounds of the particular culture from which they spring.

In other words, culture, like race, is little more than a superstition for most whites; the word, defined in a manner that sets the idea of the great white West over actual fact, holds them all in a tight fraternity. Vested interests are certainly a part of their reluctance to move outside their narrowly defined conception of culture. For if a culture means a whole way of life and if its intellectual works are only the reflections of that whole, then so-called objective and universal standards are no more than the tastes and inclinations of those engaged in one way of life. In this sense, the standards of white Americans are neither objective nor universal; they are simply subjective and white.

To accept this, however, would be for whites to admit that

---

[9] Etheridge Knight, "Hard Rock Returns to Prison from the Hospital for the Criminal Insane," in *Poems from Prison* (Detroit, 1968), pp. 11–12.

the world does not begin with Homer; they would have to realize that they are dealing with only a minute fraction of the best the world has to offer; and they would be forced—which is most to the point—to realize that the world is not composed of white supermen producing culture and nonwhite underdogs and colonial subjects attempting to rival white culture. But white literature, white art, white architecture, white philosophy, and white patterns of social organization are seldom looked upon by white intellectuals as anything but the best that has been thought and said in the world. And for countless years, as products of those lobotomizing machines established by whites (and exposed in Ralph Ellison's *Invisible Man*), many black men were willing to let such an evaluation stand. When we take a less slanted view of culture, however, we can see that the white world's definition will not do. In fact, it is to a great extent the culture theorizing of whites that has made for a separate and distinctive black American culture. That is to say, one index of the distinctiveness of black American culture is the extent to which it repudiates the culture theorizing of the white Western world; that such a repudiation is not made in any significant degree within the white world goes without saying; there are too many vested interests that militate against any dispersion of the fraternity made possible by white culture theorizing.

Folklore and Literature

We are brought back then to the history, to the question "What is America to me?" and to the most supportable answer the black American can give—"something apart." America as the refuge of huddled masses yearning to be free; America as a domain of boundless frontier; America as freedom's dream castle—these are the components of the white culture theorizer's perspective. The black perspective is another thing altogether. The masses are huddled in dark holds; the domain is one of endless slavery; and the domicile is one of bigotry's major fortresses. The two cultures that proceed out of these differing perspectives are polarized, and the bodies of intellectual and imaginative work that reflect these different cultures—while their artistic forms merge at times—stand in striking contrast to one another. A brief look at the literary aspect of the body of intellectual and imaginative work reflecting black American culture serves to illustrate the marked differences.

Brought to America in chains, put to the most degrading tasks imaginable, set outside the laws, and worked "from can to can't," black Americans were not likely to produce the same type of folklore that white America produced. Black folklore and the black American literary tradition that grew out of it are the products of a people who began in slavery and who, to a large extent, remain in slavery. Black folklore does not deal primarily with derring-do like that of Davy Crockett and Mike Fink; instead, we find the cunning and guise of Brer Rabbit or the artful gymnastics of Buck or John. Black folklore reflects the Southern agrarian environment that served as the first home of black Americans. The lore is filled with the flora and fauna of a new world as it was seen through the eyes of an enslaved people. The woods that symbolized vast wealth for white America represented a place of refuge from an irate master to blacks. To blacks, the roots and herbs that seasoned the dishes brought to white tables were a source of magic and power over the white master. And the animals of the forest, which were looked upon as game by white America, became symbols of human behavior to black Americans. Indeed, the first heroes of black American folklore were the animals of the surrounding forests.

Black folklore is not distinguished from other bodies of folklore in its employment of animal heroes, but the type of animal hero that emerges from black American folklore does set it apart. The chief trickster of black American folklore—Brer Rabbit— differs significantly from the trickster animals of other lores. Brer Rabbit was not simply another animal of the forest to black America; this trickster was not merely an entertainment for children, as the work of Joel Chandler Harris seems to indicate. Rather, Brer Rabbit was a projection of some of the deepest and strongest drives of the slave personality. J. Mason Brewer points out that the rabbit "actually symbolized the slave himself"; when Brer Rabbit won a victory over another animal, the slaves secretly rejoiced and imagined themselves smarter than their masters.[10] There was thus a psychological or subliminal aspect to

10 J. Mason Brewer, ed., *American Negro Folklore* (Chicago, 1968), pp. 3-4.

the early animal tales of black American folklore, an aspect that
was surely supplied by the slave narrator and the slave audience.
That Harris[11] and subsequently Ambrose E. Gonzales[12] tried to
identify the animal tales of black America with Aesop and an
old Western tradition is indicative of the differentiation between
black and white culture. Any black man reading about Brer
Rabbit, any black man who knows that the rabbit tales were produced by his ancestors in slavery, realizes that this black American trickster has more to do with Denmark Vesey and Nat Turner
than with Chauntecleer and Pertelote. The rabbit is a shirker of
work, a master of disguise, and a cunning figure who wins con-
tests against much larger and stronger animals. In the general
American scheme of things, to say that he is a subversive figure
is not to engage in overstatement. We can, in fact, see Brer Rabbit as one of the first black American figures to repudiate the
culture theorizing of whites.

To turn to the tales of Buck and John, the trickster slaves, is
again to encounter repudiators of white culture theorizing. Buck
and John employ daring, resourcefulness, and a type of rude wit
to gain personal benefits. The wish-fulfillment aspects of the
trickster-slave stories are even more obvious than the psychological identification with the Brer Rabbit tales. John and Buck are
also subversive creations of black American folklore; they are
bent on changing the scheme envisioned by the white culture.
For them, the best that has been thought and said in the world is
not the latest injunction to obedience by the white master but
the clever ruse that Buck uses in order to gain his freedom.[13]

The sacred folk music of black America also contains the un-
dercurrents of repudiation that set black American culture apart.
The singing that wafted to John Pendleton Kennedy's ears on
his visit to "the quarters"[14] was not the gentle outpouring of a
contented slave. When black Americans sang their spirituals,
Pharoah was a very real person: he was the white master who sat

11 Joel Chandler Harris, *Uncle Remus: His Songs and His Sayings* (New York,
1881).
12 Ambrose E. Gonzales, *With Aesop along the Black Border* (Columbia, S. C.,
1924).
13 Arna Bontemps and Langston Hughes, eds., *The Book of Negro Folklore*
(New York, 1958), p. 68.
14 John Pendleton Kennedy, *Swallow Barn* (Philadelphia, 1832).

on the porch, whip in hand. The River Jordan was not a mystical boundary between earth and heaven: it was the very real Ohio that marked the line between slave and free states. And to "steal away" was not to go docilely home to God but to escape from the Southern land of bondage. The slow and beautiful rhythms spoke not only of another world but of the real sorrow in this world; they spoke of the bare consolations offered by the American slave system, and they rejoiced that an otherworldliness was possible for men trapped in that degrading institution.

The secular folk music of the black American expresses many of the same concerns that we witness in spirituals. In black work songs, we find ironic repudiations ("pick a bale a day") of the American system, celebrations of escapes from chain gangs, and complaints of the inhumanity of overseers. In the blues of black America, we find the themes of injustice, poverty, and oppression expressed in one of the most important art forms that the black American has produced.[15] And when we look at the religious tales, the sermons, and the conversion stories of the black American, we find many of the same themes, though the narrators, like Paul Laurence Dunbar's preacher in "An Ante-Bellum Sermon," often claim that they are merely "talkin' 'bout ouah freedom / In a Bibleistic way."[16]

Thus, repudiation is characteristic of black American folklore; and this is one of the most important factors in setting black American literature apart from white American literature. The basic literary works of black America are not tales of armed frontiersmen; there are no hymns to an American God; and there are few muscular and terrible heroes who save society with their boundless vigor and ingenuity. The armed frontiersman, the American God, and the ferocious hero were the ones who stood over the slave's back and insured his continued mortification. Out of that brutalizing experience there emerged a consummate body of folk expression. The rhythms of black music are distinctive, and it is perhaps the only unique American music. The dialect and intonation of black sermons are powerful and en-

---

15 See Ralph Ellison, "Richard Wright's Blues," in *Shadow and Act* (New York, 1964).

16 Paul Laurence Dunbar, *The Complete Poems of Paul Laurence Dunbar* (New York, 1968), p. 13.

thralling; as Mike Thelwell[17] has demonstrated, they capture
the ethos of their people as it has never been captured by a white
American. The patterns of imagery and the astute wit employed
in the folk narratives are magnificent. These and other traditional
forms of black expression have provided a firm, skillfully crafted
base for the works of subsequent black artists.

From Paul Laurence Dunbar to Don L. Lee, black literary
artists have employed the black folk base in their work, and
this helps to explain the manner in which the black American
literary tradition has grown. The theme of repudiation runs
through Dunbar's "We Wear the Mask" and is as much present
in Lee's "A Poem to Complement Other Poems." The rhythms
of the music so dominant in Langston Hughes's first volume, *The
Weary Blues,* are as vital to Ted Joans's first volume, *Black Pow-
Wow.* The dialect and intonation of black sermons and religious
tales that are very much in evidence in Zora Hurston's *Jonah's
Gourd Vine* also characterize the speeches and the autobiography
of Malcolm X. Building upon the unique body of folklore that
grew out of the slave's whole way of life, black literary works
continue to reflect the development of a distinctive black culture
on the American continent.

Black American folklore is very different from white American
folklore, but it also differs significantly from African folklore.
The same can be said for black American literature in general;
it is certainly not African, and most assuredly—as its traditional
theme of repudiation illustrates—it is not another component in
the white American literary tradition. The African hare and
Brer Rabbit—as trickster animals—are as far apart, given the
experiences out of which they grew, as Davy Crockett and Stackolee. And the same might be said in reference to the protagonist
of Richard Wright's *Native Son* and the narrator of Aimé Césaire's *Return to My Native Land.* Black folklore and the black
American literary tradition that grew out of it reflect a culture
that is distinctive both of white American and of African culture,
and therefore neither can provide valid standards by which black
American folklore and literature may be judged.

17 Mike Thelwell, "Back with the Wind: Mr. Styron and the Reverend Turner,"
in *William Styron's Nat Turner: Ten Black Writers Respond,* ed. John Henrik
Clarke (Boston, 1968).

New Directions

Having taken a brief glimpse at only the literary aspect of the body of intellectual and imaginative work produced by black America, it is easy to see why black Americans are now unequivocally repudiating the white culture theorizers of our day. Black Americans have always known that race theorizing was simply the white man's means of justifying his denial of a share of the nation's wealth to the black man. Race theorizing by whites has led black men to formulate plans for African colonization, separatist groups, and black nationalist organizations. Unequal employment, the Ku Klux Klan, lynchings, East St. Louis, restrictive covenants—all these tangible, keenly felt aspects of oppression and race theorizing have been attacked by black Americans throughout their history. But only in recent decades have black Americans launched a full-scale attack on the culture theorizing of white America: cultural nationalism has been a phenomenon of the 1950s and 1960s.

The reasons behind the emergence of cultural nationalism are too manifold to be treated here. Certainly, an increased awareness of the invidious results of culture theorizing has played a large part in the growth of a new mood among black Americans. In recent years, black Americans have realized that whites have deprived them not only of material wealth but also of invaluable facts concerning their own culture. In the past, white America has taken the most skillfully crafted and beautifully expressive artifacts of black American culture and labeled them "American"; thus jazz is viewed as "America's gift to the world." Well, that just is not so; jazz, like the rich folklore, the skilled literature, and the countless other facets of the body of intellectual and imaginative work reflecting black American culture, is simply not America's to give. Black jazz, folklore, and literature proceed out of an experience that is unknown to most white Americans; they are products of a culture that white America has chosen to ignore, misrepresent, or deny. Call it black, Afro-American, Negro, the fact remains that there is a fundamental, qualitative difference between it and white American culture. Plato, E. M. Forster, Baudelaire, and many others at the heart

of what white America calls culture have only the remotest connection with black American culture.

First, black American culture was developed orally or musi-
cally for many years; the innovations of Gutenberg and Caxton,
whose effects Marshall McLuhan has attacked in recent years,
had little influence on the early expressions of black American
culture. Second, black American culture was never characterized
by the individualistic ethos of white American culture; brought
to America in shackles and placed in a society where all technology and wealth were in the hands of whites, black Americans
had little opportunity to participate in American dreams of
rugged individualism or fantasies of individual advancement.
Black American culture is characterized by a collectivistic ethos;
society is not viewed as a protective arena in which the individual
can work out his own destiny and gain a share of America's
benefits by his own efforts. To the black American these benefits
are not attained solely by individual effort, but by changes in
the nature of society and the social, economic, and political advancement of a whole race of people; society, for obvious reasons,
is seldom seen as a protective arena. The final point is one we
have already discussed at length: black American culture is
partially differentiated from white American culture because
one of its most salient characteristics is an index of repudiation.
Oral, collectivistic, and repudiative—each of these aspects helps
to distinguish black American culture from white American
culture.

There are, of course, those who insist on a unanimity of the
two cultures; they say to black America, "We are all from the
same land, and the *forms* of your intellectual and imaginative
works are the same as ours." Yes, we are all from the same land;
but, to go back to the beginning, one must realize that you came
as pilgrims and I came as a "negre." Yes, the forms of our intellectual and imaginative works do coincide at points, but the
experiences that are embodied in those forms are vastly different;
in fact, the experiences embodied in some of the forms of black
American culture explicitly repudiate the whole tradition out
of which those forms grew. And there is no contradiction here.
Kept illiterate for years by the laws of the land, the black American started where he could, with a few approved Western forms.
But a John Coltrane solo has little to do with Western forms;

LeRoi Jones's latest poems are so far from the West that white Americans just shake their heads in disbelief; and William Kelley's *Dunfords Travels Everywheres* ends on notes that the white West is hard pressed to comprehend.

The lobotomizing is over. The question "What is America to me?" has been answered by black America with a great deal of certainty in recent years. We are no longer what Calvin Hernton has called "self-riddled" blacks;[18] the sense of "twoness" that Du Bois handles so skillfully in *The Souls of Black Folk* is fast disappearing as cultural nationalism grows stronger. The doubts, speculations, and reflections are falling into a clear and ordered pattern, and we realize that America is something apart. The boundaries of our nation are marked by the color of our skin, Harold Cruse tells us,[19] and we are willing to accept his assessment. When the history is submitted to a just scrutiny, its clear and hard facts speak of the marked difference between the whole way of life of the black man and the whole way of life of the white man. Fully aware of white America's denials, fully aware that white America's talk of race differentiation is sheer superstition, black Americans are now engaged in a rejuvenating examination of the body of intellectual and imaginative work that reflects their own unique culture. The numbing electric shocks are at an end, and we are feeling completely well.

[18] Calvin Hernton, "Dynamite Growing out of Their Skulls," in *Black Fire*, ed. LeRoi Jones and Larry Neal (New York, 1968), p. 84.

[19] Harold Cruse, "Revolutionary Nationalism and the Afro-American," in *Black Fire*, ed. Jones and Neal, p. 44.

II Black Folklore and
the Black American Literary Tradition

I

THE existing monuments form an ideal order among them
selves," said T. S. Eliot, for whom the ideal order and it
modifications constituted a definition of tradition in a
somewhat restricted literary sense. In this sense all works in a
body of literature combine to form the tradition of that body
and the introduction of a new work modifies the tradition as a
whole. When we turn to an exploration of the black literary
tradition, we can hardly doubt the applicability of Eliot's defi
nition. The monuments of black American literature constitute
an ideal order, and both the critic of this literature and the
writer himself must possess what Eliot called "the historica
sense"; that is to say, both must recognize and understand the
order constituted by existing works, and both must realize where
they themselves stand in relationship to that order. At the foun
dation of the black American literary tradition stands black
folklore. To understand the order as a whole, one must first
come to terms with its foundation; this is the first step toward a
recognition of what is genuinely new in contemporary works of
black American literature.

The word *tradition*, however, has another meaning, one that
is broader, less literary. This second definition refers to customs
practices, and beliefs that have been handed down from genera
tion to generation by "the folk" or "the group." The word is nc
less valuable to us in this sense, for surely tradition in a socio
historical context plays an important role in the writer's devel
opment and in the critic's task. As Charles Sainte-Beuve noted:

Very great individuals rise beyond a group. They themselves make
a center, and gather others to them. But it is the group, the associa
tion, the alliance and active exchange of ideas, that gives to the

man of talent all his *participation in what is outside himself,* all
his maturing and value.[1]

Since the group provides direction and gives to the artist principles for the conduct of life, Sainte-Beuve felt that it was necessary for the critic to know the group in which the artist had his
genesis; in short, he believed an awareness of sociohistorical
factors was a necessity for the reader who wished fully to understand a work of art.

In this second sense of the word *tradition,* it is still black folk-
ore that rests at the foundation; for the customs, practices, and
beliefs of the black American race (of the group in which the
talented black writer has his genesis) are clearly and simply reflected in the folklore. Some initial attention to the lore aids in
an evaluation of black expression, and, paradoxically, it is early
black expression that provides one of the surest sources of this
sociohistorical knowledge.

The value of black folklore in both the literary and the sociohistorical sense of the word *tradition* forces us to come to terms
with the concept of "the folk" before we can arrive at some clear
idea of what the black literary tradition encompasses. In the
most basic sense, the term refers to all black people in America.
In a more definitive sense, however, it refers to that "unsophisticated, homogeneous group" of black people in America "living
in a politically-bounded advanced culture but isolated from it
by such factors as topography, geography, religion, dialect, economics and race."[2] Obviously topography, geography, and religion have not been as influential in the isolation of the black
folk as have dialect, economics, and race. Brought to this country for economic reasons, the first black Americans were legally
and systematically isolated on the basis of race, and their dialect
—a result of acculturation—helped to set them even further
apart. The story of the isolation of the black folk has been too
well told by such men as Benjamin Quarles, E. Franklin Frazier,
John Hope Franklin, Lerone Bennett, and others to need repetition, but it is essential to realize that this isolation was one of

[1] From "Chateaubriand," *Nouveau Lundis,* July 22, 1862. In *Criticism: The
Major Texts,* ed. Walter Jackson Bate (New York, 1952), p. 498. Italics are
Sainte-Beuve's.

[2] John Greenway, *Literature among the Primitives* (Hatboro, Pa., 1964), p. xii.

the most thorough, brutal, and complete separations that any
group has ever endured. The moral implications are not of great
concern here, but the implications for a study of black folklore
cannot be ignored.

In effect, a race was *created* from the blacks brought to America; their African ties were severed as thoroughly as possible by
slave traders, plantation owners, and politicians, and the folk
were accorded neither the rights nor the privileges of American
citizenship. Richard Wright has expressed the results of these
conditions: "Truly, you must now know that the word Negro in
America means something not racial or biological, but something purely social, something made in the United States."[3]
Just as the black American is a social being composed of racial
and cultural traits ranging from African to Irish, so his folklore
is a social product composed of elements from many stocks. The
thesis of Richard Dorson's *Negro Folktales in Michigan*, therefore, seems applicable:

> United States Negro tales form a distinctive repertoire, separate from
> the narratives of West Africa, the West Indies, Europe, the British
> Isles, and white America. Southern Negroes have drawn upon all
> these lores, and added materials from their own environment and
> experience to produce a highly diversified and culturally indepen-
> dent folk tradition.[4]

Sterling Brown has set forth the same *sui generis* category for
black spirituals that Dorson claims for black folktales, and his
explanation seems more desirable than attributing either the
songs or the tales of the black American to a specific racial or
cultural group on the basis of provenance.[5] Not that black folklore includes none of the elements of other lores; the point is
simply that out of a conglomerate of contacts has come a singular
body of folk expression which reflects a singular folk experience.
The categories are the same—animal tale, religious tale, folk
song, ballad, and so forth—but the reflected experience is unique.
Moreover, the significance of black folklore is perhaps greater
than that of any other lore in a discussion of the literary tradition

[3] Richard Wright, "The Literature of the Negro in the United States," in *White
Man, Listen!* (New York, 1964), p. 80.
[4] Cambridge, Mass., 1956, p. 187.
[5] Sterling Brown, "The Spirituals," in *The Book of Negro Folklore*, ed. Arna
Bontemps and Langston Hughes (New York, 1958), pp. 279–89.

of the race from which it originated. Even the most recent black American writer is closer to the earliest folk expression of his culture than are the recent writers of most other groups; the contemporary black author is but three hundred odd years removed, a bare modicum of time to the folklorist.

An exploration of the various genres of black folklore, therefore, should reveal the sources of some of the themes and techniques that we find in the work of conscious literary artists from Paul Laurence Dunbar to Ralph Ellison. Moreover, such an exploration should help to explain the significance of these themes and techniques and should carry us toward a further awareness of the presence of the past.

II Animal Tales

One of the most widely known genres of black folklore is the animal tale. The earliest collector and popularizer of black animal tales was Joel Chandler Harris, whose first volume, *Uncle Remus: His Songs and His Sayings,* was published in 1881; subsequent volumes appeared for the rest of the author's life. His work and the work of his immediate followers, however, while it is of undoubted value, does not truly represent black folk values. Harris and his contemporaries adopted an antebellum perspective and put black animal tales in the mouth of a faithful black retainer—a simple, primitive child of nature. It is not surprising that Harris and others depicted white plantation children as this puerile narrator's audience.

In fact, black animal tales are similar in some respects to the animal tales of all other lores. That is to say, they began as etiological stories and accrued meaning as time passed.[6] From the earliest stages of his existence, man has had a keen interest in animals (if not out of intellectual curiosity, at least for self-interest), and his observations of their actions together with his lack of scientific knowledge has led him to evolve tales of explanation. The explanatory nature of the animal tale was ideally suited to the needs of the black folk in America, since the land

[6] Alexander Haggerty Krappe, *The Science of Folklore* (New York, 1930), pp. 50–63.

and its fauna were alien to the founders of the black American
race. Moreover, given the lack of sophistication of the black folk
in relation to the advanced culture that surrounded them, one
would expect to find a high incidence of animal tales in their
folklore. The farther back we go in time, "the more conspicuou
becomes the place taken by etiological animal tales."[7]

As time passed, however, black animal tales took on new
meaning, moving closer to the fable. They lost part of their ex
planatory character and came to be employed more for enter
tainment and instruction. The chief character of the black ani
mal tales, Brer Rabbit, is an entertaining figure who had much
wisdom to impart to the black folk. J. Mason Brewer delineate
the trickster rabbit as follows:

> The role of the rabbit in the tales of the American Negro is simila
> to that of the hare in African folk narratives—that of the trickste
> who shrewdly outwits and gains a victory over some physicall
> stronger or more powerful adversary. The animal tales told by Negre
> slaves with Brer Rabbit as the hero had a meaning far deeper tha
> mere entertainment. The rabbit actually symbolized the slave him
> self. Whenever the rabbit succeeded in proving himself smarter tha
> another animal the slave rejoiced secretly, imagining himself smarte
> than his master.[8]

Black animal tales, therefore, resemble the animal tales of othe
lores in their employment of the trickster, but the social condi
tion of the folk producing them gives an added dimension,
certain psychical component which the slave narrator surely sup
plied and which his slave audience readily recognized.

The subliminal component of black animal tales is apparent
in the delineation of the trickster as a cunning figure who trick
others into doing his work. The "avoidance of work" situation
motivates the action of such tales as "Playing Godfather," "Ta
Baby," and "Brer Fox and the Goobers."[9] In each of these tale
Brer Rabbit sets out to evade work, and in the process tricks th
larger animals, escapes punishment, and even comes away with
certain material gains. Both "Playing Godfather" and "Ta

---

[7] *Ibid.*, p. 61.

[8] J. Mason Brewer, *American Negro Folklore* (Chicago, 1968), pp. 3–4.

[9] The tales, sermons, testimonials, songs, and ballads used for illustrative pur
poses in my text may be found in Bontemps and Hughes, *The Book of Negr*
Folklore.

Baby" have parallels in other lores,[10] but the very title of "Brer Fox and the Goobers," indicates its proximity to the black folk, since *goober* ("peanut") is an African linguistic survival.

A second trait of the black animal tale—the hero's employment of disguises—reflects what must have been a familiar experience. In both "The Watcher Blinded" and "Why Brer Gator's Hide Is So Horny," Brer Rabbit shows his expertise in deception. After they had killed a stolen ox, "rabbit asked wolf what would he do if some ladies came and asked him for some meat." When the wolf answers that he would give it to them free of charge, the rabbit begins his performance. The stupidity of the wolf is emphasized by the fact that Brer Rabbit assumes four different feminine disguises and receives a portion of the wolf's meat each time. In "Why Brer Gator's Hide Is So Horny," the protagonist conceals his feelings about Brer Gator in order to trick the larger animal into a painful situation, one which alters the gator's perspective as well as his appearance.

A third trait of black animal tales—the ambivalent attitude toward the trickster—is shared by the animal tales of all lores.[11] Brer Rabbit is not always the cunning and successful hero; he is often depicted as a coarse blunderer. "The Watcher Blinded" shows Brer Rabbit jeopardizing himself in an act of lyrical bragadocio; the "Tar Baby" story shows the trickster tricked; and in "Why Brer Rabbit Wears a 'Round-'Bout" the hero is brought to a painful end. In all lores, these stories reflect the fact that while the narrator and the audience admire the trickster's cunning, they also envy his prowess and fear its possible ramifications.

Black animal tales thus contain both the universal aspects of the animal tale genre and certain characteristic aspects that mark them as the product of the black American folk experience. The common traits of the trickster are present, but his identification with the slave makes the tales unique. Like all animal tales, those in black folklore proceed out of a sylvan and agrarian environment, but they also proceed out of a slave experience in which the success or failure of the trickster had a singularly important didactic and wish-fulfillment value.

[10] Cf. Aurelia Espinosa, "Notes on the Origin and History of the Tar-Baby Story," *Journal of American Folklore*, XLIII (1930), pp. 129–209.

[11] Greenway, p. 72.

The agrarianism and didactism of black animal tales connect this genre with another genre of black folklore, the proverb.[12] Although they are not uniquely black in theme, black proverbs seem to come directly out of the agrarian soil that nourished the black American race, and the idiom in which they are expressed marks them as distinctively black. Proverbs like "Tarrypin walk fast 'nuff fer to go visitin'," or "Rooster makes mo racket dan de hin w'at lay de aig," or "Hongry rooster don't cackle w'en he fine a wum" are obviously close to the black animal tale in many respects, and the psychical element noted in the animal tales may have been present even in these terse reflections.

III The Trickster Slave

In black folklore, the tales surrounding the exploits of the trickster slave are known as the "John Cycle." John or Jack, or whatever name the protagonist may assume, is usually presented as a lazy, affable slave who has a somewhat easy relationship with his master and is incessantly engaged in some contest with him. Although there are stories which present him as the loser and show him in the throes of punishment, in most cases he emerges victorious, sometimes even gaining his freedom. Tales of the trickster slave began to appear after the Civil War, and the degree of impunity enjoyed by the black folk narrator after the war probably helped to account for the substitution of Jack or John for Brer Rabbit. In the days of jubilee and freedom, the black narrator could talk of the black man's subversion and trickery with a reasonable degree of safety. The trickster in the John tales, therefore, became overtly identified with the black slave. Dorson delineates the tales in the following manner:

Folktale critics who see the Rabbit as the psychic symbol of Negro resentment against the white man cannot know of the crafty slave named John. Seldom printed, the spate of stories involving John and his Old Master provides the most engaging theme in American Negro lore. . . . trickster John directly expresses and illuminates the plantation Negro character. No allegoric or symbolic creation, he is a generic figure representing the ante-bellum slave who enjoyed some measure of favoritism and familiarity with his owner.[13]

12 Brewer, *American Negro Folklore*, p. 28.
13 Dorson, p. 49.

It is not true that the critic who sees Brer Rabbit as a psychic symbol must be ignorant of the John tales; John is a later figure, and attitudes, impossible earlier, had a good deal to do with his appearance.

The action of the trickster slave tales is made possible only by a lowering of the barriers that normally separated the master and the slave. In "A Laugh That Meant Freedom," for example, Nehemiah is free to come in contact with his various masters, and he is allowed the opportunity to jest with them. It is Nehemiah's ability to jest that helps him avoid work and that eventually secures his liberty. In "How Buck Won His Freedom," Buck's opportunity to steal from the master without fear of a whipping (or death) is made possible by the master's tolerance, since many masters felt that the petit larceny of the slave functioned as an escape valve for his aggression. In this tale, it is finally the master's overconfidence, combined with the slave's knowledge of white society's vulnerabilities, that enables Buck to win his freedom. The stupidity of the master is driven home by the fact that after allowing Buck's knowledge to become consummate he is foolish enough to challenge the slave; the results of the contest are predetermined.

The trickster slave, however, is not always presented as the daring, resourceful challenger of the system; at times he is simply a clownish fellow who escapes defeat through crude wit and uncommon luck. The protagonist of "Uncle Israel and the Law" possesses a desire for material gain that almost lands him in jail. "Do you know who I am?" asks the stranger to whom Uncle Israel has told fantastic tales of chicken stealing. "No, sah, Boss, 'ceptin' yuh's a chicken buyah. Who else is Yuh?" "I'm the biggest constable in this county," answers the stranger. The trickster seems trapped, but his quick wit effects his escape. "Sez yuh is, Boss? Wal, Ah'll decla'. An' don' yuh know who Ah is? Ain't Massa and de oberseeah tol' yuh who Ah is? Wal, Ah's de bigges' liah in dis county." In "The Prophet Vindicated," a combination of proverbial wisdom and luck allows Uncle Phimon to triumph. When Phimon, who had claimed he could prophesy the future and see things hidden from ordinary men, is put to a test, he finally admits his frauds with the words, "Wal, Massa, de ol' coon run uh long time, but dey cotch 'im at las." His hearers fail to realize that he is making a confession, however, and when the box whose contents he was supposed to divine is turned over, an old coon scampers out.

Beyond their wish-fulfillment value, trickster slave tales also seem to represent a romanticizing of the slave experience, from a black antebellum perspective. The tales appeared immediately after the Civil War, and a general romanticizing of the "Old South" began as soon as the defeat of the Confederacy became apparent. In the "John Cycle," masters are tolerant and kind, and the slave is allowed rights that could not have been "inalienable" in a slave system. Considering the plight of the freedman, however, it is not surprising that some of the wandering, hungry, and jobless folk looked back on slavery as a time of security and happiness. But the sentimental elements of the trickster tales cannot obscure the fact that they are tales of rebellion, tales of the subversion of the slave system by the jester slave.

From this examination it seems as though some redefinition of the traditional feat and contest heroes is in order when we are dealing with black folklore, for when we consider the folk background of the black race, the stakes in the animal and trickster tales are similar to those in the European romances and legendary ballads. The contest or feat hero of European and other lores wages a battle which must result in freedom or gain on one side and death or incarceration on the other. If we consider the subliminal element of black animal tales and the aspect of ego projection in the John Cycle, we can see this same dichotomy. The trickster (although a slave) had as much to lose if he was defeated as Jason—or Pecos Bill. The trickster of black folklore is both a feat and a contest hero, since in his own manner he fights impressive battles and accomplishes impressive feats, given the nature of his environment. An understanding of the experience of the black American folk and of the psychical component of their tales makes it less difficult for us to see how a hero who not only endured but also achieved certain material gains assumes the status of a quest, contest, or feat hero. Thus it is impossible to agree with the limited view of critics who ignore these crucial aspects of the tales: "On reading through the large body of recorded Negro folktales, one is struck by the one-sided preference for trickster heroes as compared to the well-developed tradition of quest and defender heroes found in abundance in the traditions of the Indians and whites living in close contact with the Negroes."[14] There is no striking or one-sided preference apparent in the tales if one sees the trickster as the contest or feat hero that he surely was for the black folk; what is needed is a modification of Orin Klapp's extremely helpful article on the folk hero,[15] a modification that would take full account of what Sainte-Beuve called the "group" that provides the maturing and value for the artist.

Before leaving the initial stages of folk expression, it should be noted that an extensive body of superstitions, ghost stories, witch-riding stories, voodoo tales, and "hant" stories also characterize black folklore. The same lack of detailed knowledge that contributed to the emergence of the animal tale also motivated explanatory tales that were wider ranging. Witches, hants, and ghosts helped to explain unusual happenings—radical changes of personality, mysterious sicknesses, or merely noises in the night. Voodoo, the practice of attempting to control events by the use of charms, spells, or rituals, was similar to magic, but its implications were more ominous, since the voodoo doctor or the conjurer in the tales often inflicted death or injury on his victims. In some communities both voodoo and conjure reached the religious level. "Superstition," as Krappe points out, "in common parlance designates the sum of beliefs and practices shared by other people in so far as they differ from our own. What we believe and practise ourselves is, of course, religion."[16]

IV   Religious Tales, Preacher Tales,
Sermons, and Testimonials

The church has played a singular role in the development of black American culture. In one sense, it precedes the family as a black cultural institution, for the black family as such did not exist during the days of slavery. The church was the first stable black institution in America; it was the center of religious, social,

---

14 Fred O. Weldon, Jr., "Negro Folktale Heroes," in *And Horns on the Toads*, ed. Mody C. Boatwright, Wilson M. Hudson, Allen Maxwell (Dallas, 1959), p. 170.
15 Orin E. Klapp, "The Folk Hero," *Journal of American Folklore*, LXI (1949), pp. 17–25.
16 Krappe, p. 203.

and political activity and produced many of the most dynamic black leaders. Its importance is adequately reflected in black folklore, where we find an extensive body of religious tales, preacher tales, sermons, and testimonials, all of which are both didactic and entertaining.

One familiar quip characterizes black religion as opposed to white in the following manner:

> White folks go to Chu'ch
> He nevah crack a smile
> Nigguh go to Chu'ch
> You heah 'im laff a mile.[17]

All that is simple, however, is not naive; for this statement contains an essential fact of religious history. From time immemorial preachers, prophets, and religious leaders have recognized the value of entertaining the audience. The effectiveness of the simple, entertaining story is perhaps greatest when basic religious truths are being imparted. The exemplum aided the medieval religious teacher in his dealings with the peasantry of England, and the short, illustrative religious tale occupies some place in the history of most religions of the world.

In black folklore, we find a story like "De Ways of de Wimmens," functioning as an explanatory, didactic, and entertaining tale. Its stated purpose is to explain the nature of femininity—an awesome task in any age—but the tale goes further than this. It provides an explication of the Genesis story, showing man his place in the universe, and it provides more than one laugh. In effect, it renders an exegesis that is sufficiently imaginative to be understood by an unsophisticated audience. The beginning paragraph of the tale perhaps best illustrates why it would appeal to folk listeners: "Most folks say de six day was Satdy, cause on de SEVENTH day didn't de Lawd rest an look his creation over? Now hit MAY be Satdy dat he done de WORK of making man an woman, but from all de signs, he must THOUGHT UP de first man an woman on old unlucky FRIDAY." The body of the tale details how Adam gained strength while Eve gained control of the keys to the kitchen and the bedroom as gifts from "de Lawd." The ending offers memorable humor: "So dat de reason, de very reason, why de mens THINKS dey is de boss and de wimmen KNOWS dey is boss, cause dey got dem two little keys to use in dat slippery wimmen's way. Yas, fawever mo an den some! And if you don't know DAT already, you ain't no married man."

Another type of religious tale stands in antithesis to the exemplum. In black folklore it is known as the preacher tale. The religious leader has been the protagonist of amusing (at times, scandalous) stories for ages, and the black preacher is no exception. Brewer explains that "the preacher has always been the acknowledged leader in the Negro community, and as such he has been the target of many witty stories told by his followers."[18] And Dorson says of the protagonists of preacher tales, "Their alleged pomposity, greed, unchastity, and hypocrisy made fine joke material for the humour of deflation and irreverence."[19]

Narratives such as "The Farmer and G.P.C.," "The Preacher and His Farmer Brother," and "Reverend Carter's Twelfth Anniversary Sermon" display the humor of deflation in abundance. The farmer's willingness to "go preach Christ" is quickly deflated by the more practical woman who reads the initial *G.P.C.*, which the clouds seem to form, as "go pick cotton." The piety of the preacher, which leads him to attribute his brother's fine crops to "de Lawd," is punctured by the brother's timely remark, "Yeah, but you oughta seed hit when de Lawd had it by Hisse'f." And the otherworldly reverence of preachers receives a prick when the spry Reverend Carter dances on Sunday for a fee and promises to do the same every Sunday if a similar reward is forthcoming. In each of these tales, the church leader is pulled down from his godly perch and shown in all his essential humanity.

But if the preacher himself was often the target of humorous abuse, his sermon was a different matter altogether. The sermon was considered "de Word" of God revealed to man, and in its imagery, detail, and sheer poetry, the black sermon is uniquely powerful. The sermons display the same literalness and picturesqueness of speech that Dobie has noted as characteristic of the religious tales;[20] they present a vivid picture of a personal God

[18] *Ibid.*, p. 3.
[19] Dorson, p. 166.
[20] J. Frank Dobie, "A Word on *The Word*," in Brewer, *The Word on the Brazos*, pp. ix–x.

and a "chosen people" in language that is often startling in its grace. One of the most famous black sermons, John Jasper's "De Sun Do Move," contains striking images: "I don't carry de keys to de Lord's closet and He ain't tell me to peep in and if I did I'm so stupid I wouldn't know it when I see it"; "But I can read de Bible and get de things what lay on de top of de soil"; "Truth is mighty; it can break de heart of stone and I must fire another arrow of truth out of de quiver of de Lord." The imagery of "The Wounds of Jesus," a sermon recorded by Zora Neale Hurston, is equally impressive: "When de blood is lopin thru yo' veins/Like de iron monasters [monsters] on de rail"; "Two thousand years have went by on their rusty ankles"; "From the stroke of the master's axe/One angel took the flinches of God's eternal power/And bled the veins of the earth." Images such as these speak of the vitality, literalness, and closeness to the soil of the people who produced them; they speak, moreover, of a people who believed in the nearness of God, in his personal nature, in his graciousness and his power. Black sermons, in short, constitute some of the finest poetry of belief ever written, and their fusion of the earthly and the abstract makes them pulsate with meaning.

Another form of religious tale is the black testimonial, which displays some of the same techniques seen in the sermons. The imagery of the opening lines of the testimonial, "God Struck Me Dead," for example—"I have always been a sheep. I was never a goat. I was created and cut out and born in the world for Heaven" —is so brilliant that it immediately captures our attention, and using a favorite device of the black preacher, it identifies the speaker from the outset as one of God's company. The testimonial continues by carrying us into a world of significant numbers, dream visions, and miraculous cures, offering an example of mystical writing of the first order. Yet it is distinguished from a more learned mystical tradition in its employment of the most mundane, at times agrarian, imagery. The work conveys the light and dark of the conversion experience and all of its ramifications in a beautifully simple, poetic manner:

When God struck me dead with His power I was living on 14th Avenue. It was the year of the Centennial. I was in my house alone and I declare unto you when His power struck me I died. I fell out on the floor flat on my back. I could neither speak nor move for my tongue stuck to the roof of my mouth; my jaws were locked and my limbs were stiff.

Such language could not have failed to affect a godly, or even an ungodly, audience.

V Folk Songs

The songs of black folklore can be categorized under two headings—sacred and secular. In the first category we find the black spirituals, and in the second, the work, levee, river, boating, sea, and jubilee songs. The cogency, beauty, and power of the black spirituals, however, put them first in any evaluation of black folk songs. Spirituals were the first items of black folklore to be collected and publicized with a degree of seriousness. Thomas Wentworth Higginson, an early collector, commented on the nature of the spirituals and recorded a number of them in an article in the *Atlantic* (1867) and in the later *Army Life in a Black Regiment* (1870). W. F. Allen and others familiar with the life and songs of the Sea Islanders of South Carolina published in 1867 a collection of spirituals entitled *Slave Songs of the United States*. Allen's introduction to the volume is still valuable as a guide to the songs. A host of other collectors have written about the spirituals, and although they have debated the origins of the songs, they have usually accorded them high praise.

The controversy over the origin of the spirituals, precipitated and nourished by Henry Krehbiel, James Weldon Johnson, and others, seems best resolved by Sterling Brown's comment: "Neither European nor African, but partaking of elements of both, the result is a new kind of music, certainly not mere imitation, but more creative and original than any other American music."[21] Despite the fact that they grow out of and employ the vocabulary, prophecies, and stories of a Protestant tradition, there is nothing in the history of American religious and secular music to equal the poignancy and lyricism of the black spirituals. The

21 Brown, p. 284.

songs, in fact, are almost unique in the history of America, as W. E. B. Du Bois has pointed out:

Little of beauty has America given the world save the rude grandeur of God himself stamped on her bosom; the human spirit in this new world has expressed itself in vigor and ingenuity rather than in beauty. And so by fateful chance the Negro folk-song—the rhythmic cry of the slave—stands to-day not simply as the sole American music, but as the most beautiful expression of human experience born this side of the seas.[22]

Like all accomplished works of art, the spirituals show many sides; they are as complex and difficult to define as the word *beauty*. On one hand—considering spirituals such as "Go Down Moses," "Mary Don't You Weep," and "Steal Away"—one can see that the black religious folk identified themselves with the chosen people of Israel. Going further, however, we can see a subversive aspect in the spirituals; after all, Pharoah's army did get drowned. To "steal away," moreover, was anything but constructive for the plantation economy, and when freedom's chariot came low, there were normally fewer slaves in the field the next morning.

On the other hand, the spirituals manifest a great and abiding sorrow, as anyone who has heard "Nobody Knows the Trouble I've Seen," "I Know Moonrise," or "Motherless Child" well sung can testify. In these songs, we have "the articulate cry of the slave to the world," and it seems perfectly justifiable to call them "sorrow songs": the element of pathos singled out by early commentators reveals itself again and again.

But there is also joy, vitality, and a sense of black "fused strength" in spirituals like "No More Auction Block," "Deep River," and "God's Gonna Set Dis World on Fire." In these we see the promised joy of salvation and escape, and we witness one illustration of the apocalypse theme that pervades black American literature. In such songs we have both happiness and hope, and the same can be said of songs such as "When the Saints Go Marching In," "Every Time I Feel the Spirit," and "The Virgin Mary Had a Baby Boy."

The spirituals, therefore, form a genre that cannot be easily

22 W. E. B. Du Bois, "Of the Sorrow Songs," in *The Souls of Black Folk*, in *Three Negro Classics*, ed. John Hope Franklin (New York, 1965), p. 378.

categorized; through complex rhythm and crafted poetry, these songs range the entire gamut of human experience. They proceed from the heart of humanity, and their simple form—a single line of recitative and a single line of refrain—makes them memorable. A number of collectors have commented on the method of composition of the spirituals, but again it is Sterling Brown who provides one of the most elucidating statements.[23] Brown feels that the vocabulary, the idiom, and the stories of the spirituals were taken from a "folk storehouse," and that as one "leader" had exhausted his stock, another would take up the recitative. In this manner, the spirituals were not merely sung, but actually "composed," and even the simplest incidents could provide motivation for a new spiritual or could be worked into the framework of an existing one. One former slave detailed the method of composition to James McKim as follows:

I'll tell you; it's dis way. My master call me up and order me a short peck of corn and a hundred lash. My friends see it and is sorry for me. When dey come to de praise meeting dat night dey sing about it. Some's very good singers and know how; and dey work it in, work it in, you know; till dey get it right; and dat's de way.[24]

We may well conclude with McKim that this is "a very satisfactory explanation."

The secular songs of the black folk are largely concerned with the primary activity of the folk experience—work. Black work songs proceed from the chain gang, the cottonfields, the levee, the inland waterways, and the high seas. They were either accompaniments to the work or descriptions of it. Thus we have the rock-smashing rhythms of "Hyah Come de Cap'm" and "Take This Hammer," and we have the humor and subtle protest of "Pick a Bale of Cotton" (it took an able-bodied man a week, not a day as in the song, to pick a bale of cotton). The chain-gang songs protest the treatment accorded prisoners, and they frequently delineate the escaped convict—the man who has defied

---

[23] Brown, "The Spirituals," p. 281. Another notable account is James Weldon Johnson's Introduction to *The Book of American Negro Spirituals* (New York, 1969).

[24] James Miller McKim, "Negro Songs," in *The Negro and His Folklore in Nineteenth-Century Periodicals*, ed. Bruce Jackson (Austin, Tex., 1967), pp. 58–59. McKim's article originally appeared in *Dwight's Journal of Music*, XIX (1862), pp. 148–49.

the system—as a folk hero. The sea and river songs, like "Blow the Man Down," provide the rhythm for work and at the same time describe the nature of the work and the life that accompanies it.[25]

Two groups of secular songs remain: the jubilee songs and, more important, the blues. Jubilee songs were sung by the folk on celebration days, and the name, according to Maud Cuney-Hare, comes from the chief drummer—known as "Juba"—who pounded out the rhythms. The origin of the blues is not quite so simply explained, for they, in a real sense, represent the juncture of many streams of black folk song and experience. The art form of the blues is a distillate of black music and black folk experience.

A song like "See, See Rider" chronicles the promiscuity forced on blacks, male and female, by society: "I'm goin' away, baby, I won't be back till fall./Lord, Lord, Lord!/Goin' away, baby, won't be back till fall./If I find me a good man, I won't be back at all." And "Southern Blues" captures the pain of hard luck and fickle lovers:

House catch on fire
And ain't no water around,
If your house catch on fire,
Ain't no water around,
Throw yourself out the window,
Let it burn on down.

. . . . . .

Let me be your ragdoll
Until your china comes.
Let me be your ragdoll
Until your china comes.
If he keeps me ragged,
He's got to rag it some.

"Careless Love" chronicles the anguish of the casual love affairs caused by a migratory existence, and in "Good Morning Blues," appears the overall attitude of endurance in the face of despair:

[25] Maud Cuney-Hare assigns part of her study, *Negro Musicians and Their Music* (Washington, D.C., 1936), to black folk songs of the waterways, the levee, and the high seas, and a number of these songs are recorded in Lafcadio Hearn's "Levee Life," in Bontemps and Hughes, *The Book of Negro Folklore*, pp. 211–22.

> Good mornin', blues,
> Blues, how do you do?
> Yes, blues, how do you do?
> I'm doing all right,
> Good morning, how are you?

Throughout the genre, songs like "The Midnight Special" express what the railroad meant to the black folk as a means both of escape and of carrying love away or bringing it "back home."

Ralph Ellison's definition of the blues seems the most comprehensive and enlightening one:

The blues is an impulse to keep the painful details and episodes of a brutal experience alive in one's aching consciousness, to finger its jagged grain, and to transcend it, not by the consolation of philosophy but by squeezing from it a near-tragic, near-comic lyricism. As a form, the blues is an autobiographical chronicle of personal catastrophe expressed lyrically.[26]

Endurance and transcendence by lyricism are two of the most important aspects of the black folk experience, and the blues capture these essential aspects with consummate skill.

VI Ballads

The final genre of black folklore to be considered is the ballad. Black folk ballads are not numerous, but two are quite important in the present discussion because of their popularity and their role in the development of the black folk hero. One of these is the widely known "John Henry," and the other is "Stackolee." "John Henry" has "transcended" its classification as a black folk ballad, since the hero has become a national folk hero; and a recent rendition of "Stackolee" has increased the popularity of that ballad's protagonist.

The reason for the appeal of "John Henry" is not far to seek; the contest of the ballad is between man and machine. The ballad, of course, reflects more than a simple contest; what we have in "John Henry" is the essential dichotomy of the nineteenth-century industrial revolution and the twentieth-century age of

---

[26] Ralph Ellison, "Richard Wright's Blues," in *Shadow and Act* (New York, 1966), p. 90.

technology. The work presents the new industrial laborer who attempts to retain his importance in the face of an awesome technology, and the results of the effort are foreordained—the man is crushed:

> The steam drill was on the right han' side,
> John Henry was on the left,
> Says before I let this steam drill beat me down,
> I'll hammah myself to death,
> I'll hammah myself to death.
>
> .   .   .   .   .
>
> The hammah that John Henry swung,
> It weighed over nine poun',
> He broke a rib in his left han' side,
> And his intrels fell on the groun',
> And his intrels fell on the groun'.

Yet the protagonist is a contest or feat hero of note; his daring is not to be denied, and the pathos and sorrow that accompany his death are his just rewards.

The hero of "Stackolee," on the other hand, is anything but a pitiable figure; he is to be feared and respected because of his deviance from accepted codes of conduct:

One dark and dusty day
I was strolling down the street.
I thought I heard some old dog bark,
But it warn't nothing but Stackolee gambling in the dark.
Stackolee threw seven.
Billy said, It ain't that way.
You better go home and come back another day.
Stackolee shot Billy four times in the head
And left that fool on the floor damn near dead.
Stackolee decided he'd go up to Sister Lou's.
Said, Sister Lou! Sister Lou, guess what I done done?
I just shot and killed Billy, your big-head son.
Sister Lou said, Stackolee, that can't be true!
You and Billy been friends for a year or two.
Stackolee said, Woman, if you don't believe what I said,
Go count the bullet holes in that son-of-a-gun's head.
Sister Lou got frantic and all in a rage,
Like a tea hound dame on some frantic gage.
She got on the phone, Sheriff, Sheriff, I want you to help poor me.

I want you to catch that bad son-of-a-gun they call Stackolee.
Sheriff said, My name might begin with an *s* and end with an *f*
But if you want that bad Stackolee you got to get him yourself.
So Stackolee left, he went walking down the New Haven track.
A train come along and flattened him on his back.
He went up in the air and when he fell
Stackolee landed right down in hell.
He said, Devil, devil, put your fork up on the shelf
Cause I'm gonna run this devilish place myself.
There came a rumbling on the earth and a tumbling on the ground,
That bad son-of-a-gun, Stackolee, was turning hell around.
He ran across one of his ex-girl friends down there.
She was Chock-full-o'-nuts and had pony-tail hair.
She said, Stackolee, Stackolee, wait for me.
I'm trying to please you, can't you see?
She said, I'm going around the corner but I'll be right back.
I'm gonna see if I can't stack my sack.
Stackolee said, Susie Belle, go on and stack your sack.
But I just might not be here when you get back.
Meanwhile, Stackolee went with the devil's wife and with his
        girl friend, too.
Winked at the devil and said, I'll go with you.
The devil turned around to hit him a lick.
Stackolee knocked the devil down with a big black stick.
Now, to end this story, so I heard tell,
Stackolee, all by his self, is running hell.

Stackolee represents the badman hero who stands outside the law; he is the rebel who uses any means necessary to get what he wants.

Roger Abrahams has characterized the badman hero and distinguished him from the trickster in the following manner: "Where guile and banter are the weapons of the trickster, arrogance and disdain serve the badman. He does not aim to be a god, but rather to be the eternal man in revolt, the devil."[27] Stackolee, however, represents more particularly the folk hero from the lower echelons of city life. Like the protagonists of "Frankie Baker" and "DuPree and Betty Blues," Stackolee comes out of an urban scene—a world of pimps, prostitutes, gambling, drinking, fighting, and death. He is as far removed

[27] Roger Abrahams, "The Changing Concept of the Negro Hero," in *The Golden Log*, ed. Mody C. Boatwright, Wilson M. Hudson, Allen Maxwell (Dallas, 1962), p. 124.

from the barnyard and the fields as John Henry is from the plough and the scythe. Both are heroes of the black urban and industrial experiences.

VII

Only when we have arrived at some knowledge of the heroes and values that characterize the group in which the black writer has his genesis, can we begin to discuss the work of conscious literary artists with some degree of authority. When we turn to the first black American poet of distinction, the importance of our awareness of the folk background becomes apparent. Paul Laurence Dunbar draws directly from the "folk storehouse" for the majority of his poems and short stories; often working in what has been called the "Plantation Tradition," he produced poems that share the black antebellum perspective seen in the John Cycle. But Dunbar was not all sweetness and light, and at times (in such poems as "An Ante-Bellum Sermon" and "We Wear the Mask") we see the subversive component of the trickster tales, the protest element of the work songs, and the impudence of the heroes of the badman ballads. Dunbar, the virtual father of black American poetry, was thus in some respects a "folk" poet, and we must know the lore if we are to understand his work.

Again, we must be fully aware of the black folk experience in order to come to terms with the work of the first black American prose writer of distinction, Charles Chesnutt. Chesnutt's first significant volume was a collection of short fiction entitled *The Conjure Woman* (1899). In this work we find the beliefs and practices associated with voodoo, black magic, and superstition. The full import of stories such as "The Goophered Grapevine" and "The Gray Wolf's Ha'nt" can only be grasped when we realize the role that conjure played in the lives of the agrarian black folk. Aunt Peggy, the conjurer of the first story, and Uncle Jube, of the second, virtually determine the fate of all the characters who surround them; this, of course, is possible only because the black folk (and even those who hold them in bondage, e.g., Mars Dugal) place the greatest faith in the powers of voodoo and conjure. Chesnutt, moreover, seems to make a conscious attempt to evoke the sinister mysteriousness of conjure tales, and his carefully-delineated narrator, Uncle Julius, is a storyteller in the best tradition of black expression.

The value of a knowledge of black sermons becomes apparent when we are confronted with James Weldon Johnson's *God's Trombones* (1927), one of the most beautiful volumes of verse ever produced by a black poet. Johnson used the folk sermons as a basis for his work, but modified and altered them until he produced such imaginative and exciting poems as "The Creation," "Listen, Lord—a Prayer," and "Go Down Death—a Funeral Sermon."

Familiarity with the lower-echelon urban hero facilitates our understanding of the literature of the Harlem Renaissance. Edward Margolies has pointed out that a concern for the low-life character of the city was one of the most salient features of black expression during the 1920s,[28] and Stackolee finds his counterparts in characters such as those encountered in Claude McKay's *Home to Harlem* (1928), and even in such recent black protagonists as the narrators of Claude Brown's *Manchild in the Promised Land* and *The Autobiography of Malcolm X.* Between the work of the Harlem Renaissance and that of more recent writers stand the principal figures of Ann Petry's *The Street* (1946), Chester Himes's *If He Hollers Let Him Go* (1945), and Richard Wright's *Native Son* (1940). Wright's Bigger Thomas is a counterpart of the badman hero who subverts white morality by refusing to heed its dictates; his partial victory assures freedom and material gain, but in the end he is destroyed by an inimical environment much like that which makes an early appearance in "Frankie and Johnny" and "Stackolee."

When we turn to one of Wright's later works, *Black Boy* (1945), we can again see the importance of a knowledge of the folk tradition. According to Ralph Ellison, Wright's work is a perfect expression of blues values and techniques. Ellison's statement appears in *Shadow and Act* (1953), and in this volume Ellison himself has a good deal to say about black folklore (particularly the music). One of his predecessors was equally aware of the value of the folk blues. Both the title and the content of Langston Hughes's first volume of poetry, *The Weary Blues* (1926), indi-

[28] Edward Margolies, *Native Sons: A Critical Study of Twentieth-Century Negro American Authors* (New York, 1969), pp. 30–31.

cate that perhaps the most influential black poet of this century knew the value of the blues form. And within the last six years, one of black America's most prolific writers, LeRoi Jones, has manifested his concern for the blues form and values in his poetry and in critical works such as *Blues People* (1963) and *Black Music* (1968).

The characters, themes, and techniques of black religious lore have found their finest modern manifestation in James Baldwin's *Go Tell It on the Mountain* (1952). Baldwin, who was a boy preacher in Harlem, has used in his novel the humor of deflation seen in the preacher tales, the vivid imagery of the sermons, the form of the testimonials (with their awesome pictures of the conversion experience), and the themes of the spirituals. The title of the novel, like those of several of Baldwin's essays ("Many Thousands Gone," "The Fire Next Time"), is taken from a black spiritual.

Finally, there is Ralph Ellison's *Invisible Man*. Speaking of the craft of the black novelist in "The Art of Fiction: An Interview," Ellison says:

For us [black novelists] the question should be, What are the specific *forms* of that [black American] humanity, and what in our background is worth preserving or abandoning. The clue to this can be found in folklore, which offers the first drawings of any group's character. It preserves mainly those situations which have repeated themselves again and again in the history of any given group. It describes those rites, manners, customs, and so forth, which insure the good life, or destroy it; and it describes those boundaries of feeling, thought, and action which that particular group has found to be the limitation of the human condition. It projects this wisdom in symbols which express the group's will to survive; it embodies those values by which the group lives and dies. These drawings may be crude but they are nonetheless profound in that they represent the group's attempt to humanize the world. It's no accident that great literature, the products of individual artists, is erected upon this humble base.[29]

Dryden's comment on Chaucer—"Here is God's plenty"—offers a fitting characterization of *Invisible Man*. Ellison's protagonist is both a trickster and an urban, industrial feat hero, and his

29 Ralph Ellison, "The Art of Fiction: An Interview," in *Shadow and Act*, p. 172.

adventures carry him through almost every phase of the black folk experience. There is the melancholy and promiscuity of the blues; the humor, pathos, and conversion of religious lore; the protest spirit of the work songs and the badman ballads; and the subversiveness of the animal tales and spirituals.

To understand the classic works of black literature, a knowledge of the existing monuments and of the group in which the writers had their genesis is a necessity. Black folklore stands at the base of the black literary tradition, and we must first attain a knowledge of the lore; with such knowledge comes a better understanding of the black literary tradition as a whole.

More than fifty years ago James Weldon Johnson asked some of the same questions about the composers of the spirituals that critics today are posing in regard to all major black American writers:

> O black and unknown bards of long ago,
> How came your lips to touch the sacred fire?
> How, in your darkness, did you come to know
> The power and beauty of the minstrel's lyre?

Black folklore provides many of the answers.

III Freedom and Apocalypse
A Thematic Approach to Black Expression

I

God's gonna set dis world on fire,
God's gonna set dis world on fire,
Some o' dese days. God knows it!
God's gonna set dis world on fire,
Some o' dese days.

THIS first stanza from a well known spiritual offers an early example of black America's concern with eschatology, and the final events prophecied by its lyrics seem in keeping with a Protestant religious tradition. Genesis (6–8) contains a description of the apocalyptic flood that first purged the earth of sinners, and tells how, when the waters receded, Noah received the sign of the rainbow from a vengeful God—the next purification would not come by water. The Revelation of Saint John the Divine presents the most vivid and comprehensive images of the predicted second destruction of the world:

The first angel sounded and there followed hail and fire mingled with blood, and they were cast upon the earth: and the third part of trees were burnt up, and all green grass was burnt up. And the second angel sounded, and as it were a great mountain burning with fire was cast into the sea: and the third part of the sea became blood.

One has only to read the sermons of early Puritan divines, the eighteenth-century revival preachings of Jonathan Edwards, and the awe-inspiring messages of nineteenth-century Methodist ministers to see the continual employment of such apocalyptic images by American religious leaders. At the conclusion of one of his most famous sermons, "Sinners in the Hands of an Angry God" (1741), an impassioned Edwards cries out:

O sinner! consider the fearful danger you are in. 'Tis a great furnace of wrath, a wide and bottomless pit, full of the fire of wrath, that you are held over in the hand of that God whose wrath is provoked and incensed as much against you as against many of the damned in hell. You hang by a slender thread, with the flames of divine wrath flashing about it, and ready every moment to singe it and burn it assunder; and you have no interest in any Mediator, and nothing to keep off the flames of wrath, nothing of your own, nothing that you ever have done, nothing that you can do, to induce God to spare you one moment.

Black American Spirituals such as "God's Gonna Set Dis World on Fire," "I Got a Home in Dat Rock," "Where Shall I Be When the First Trumpet Sound" and sermons delivered by such black ministers as George Liele, Black Harry, Andrew Bryan, and John Jasper make use of images much like those of Edwards. Similarities between the black and the white American's concern with eschatology and striking apocalyptic imagery are not surprising when one considers that "from the beginning of the importation of slaves into the colonies, Negroes received Christian baptism."[1] In *The Negro Church in America*, E. Franklin Frazier develops the thesis that the West African's social bonds, traditional bases of social cohesion, and means of relating to the world were virtually destroyed by the manner in which he was enslaved in America; the black church, according to Frazier, provided a new basis of social cohesion—a nation within a nation for the black American folk.[2]

Frazier's thesis, which stresses a total loss of African identity, deserves some qualification since scholars such as W. E. B. Du Bois (*The Negro*, 1915), Melville J. Herskovits (*The Myth of the Negro Past*, 1941), and others have demonstrated that black American culture contains distinct African social and religious survivals. Frazier is nevertheless correct when he asserts that the enslavement of the black man resulted in his "social and moral isolation in American society."[3] John Greenway defines a folk as an "unsophisticated, homogeneous group" isolated from a politically-bounded advanced culture by such factors as topography, geography, religion, dialect, economics and race.[4] The black folk on small farms, on large plantations, and in the cities of America,

---

[1] E. Franklin Frazier, *The Negro Church in America* (New York, 1969), p. 6.

[2] *Ibid.*, pp. 1–9 and 44.

[3] *Ibid.*, p. 44.

[4] John Greenway, *Literature among the Primitives* (Hatboro, Pa., 1964), p. xii.

having been effectively isolated from West African culture, were denied meaningful participation in white culture by proscriptive and dehumanizing laws. Thus, while the majority of Americans, both black and white, were Protestant Christians and deemed the Bible a major source of authority, religion had an import for blacks that must have been alien to most whites. Although one is forced to admit that Protestantism served the master class in its attempts to shift the slave's gaze from the brutalities of the temporal world to the rewards of the hereafter and that some slaves willingly accepted such a shift, one must also realize that black religion has always been more than a meliorative institution serving the ends of the enslaver or a placebo handed by whites to credulous blacks.

White Americans looked to religion for—among other things—future heavenly reward, guidance in day-to-day life, sanction for capitalistic enterprise, and authority to conquer wild and virgin lands. The isolated black folk, however, looked to religion as a unifying myth which could provide social cohesion. David Gordon defines such a myth as the integration of various symbols in a total view that provides a people with a "comprehensive interpretation of their past in order to inspire them with a sense of destiny."[5] Black Americans integrated the symbols of the Bible and adopted the past of the Israelites in order to link themselves with a new historical continuum when their African continuum was broken by the slave trade. The recognition of this unifying myth entails viewing the folk as subjects on a historical stage rather than as objects in the white historian's perspective on Africa and America, where blacks often find themselves portrayed as bestial, passive, and unheroic.

A remark by Jeanette Robinson Murphy, an early commentator on the spirituals, helps to clarify the slaves' assumption of a Christian past:

One of the most persistent fancies that the old slaves cherished was that they were the oppressed Israelites, that the Southerners were the cruel Egyptians, and that Canaan was freedom. Bondage was of course their slavery. They believed that some day the Red Sea would

5 David Gordon, *Self-Determination and History in the Third World* (Princeton, N.J., 1971), pp. 90–91.

come in a sea of blood, which was verified in the Civil War. In many of their songs they appropriate Bible prophecies and ideas to themselves.[6]

In many ways Christianity fulfilled black Americans' desire for a history, an identity, and a metaphysics that would meliorate the bleakness of their isolation in the New World. It was easier for a black man to awaken at day clean with his "mind set on freedom" if he believed an omnipresent God had ended the captivity and isolation of a people with whom he genuinely identified. Thus, many blacks expressed sentiments like those voiced by Paul Laurence Dunbar's antebellum preacher, who first cautions his congregation "I'm still a-preachin' ancient,/I ain't talkin' 'bout to-day," but goes on to say:

> But I tell you, fellah christuns,
> Thing'll happen mighty strange;
> Now, de Lawd done dis fu' Isrul,
> An' his ways don't nevah change.[7]

The slaves' identification with the Israelites led them to a type of black messianism—a feeling that they were the chosen people whom God would deliver from the cruel oppressors. This view, of course, necessitated a repudiation of the "slaveholding religion" and its standard texts: "Servants, obey your masters" and "He who knoweth his master's will and doeth it not shall be beaten with many stripes." In William Wells Brown's *Clotel*, one character comments on the irony of such a religion: "I think de people dat made de Bible was great fools. . . . Cause dey made such a great big book and put nuttin' in it, but servants obey yer masters."[8] Lewis Hayden, the fugitive slave and black abolitionist, noted the same irony before the Massachusetts legislature in 1855 and went on to call for a different type of religion: "Yes— the missionary and the slave priest stand up side by side and say 'Servants, obey your masters,' and such like gospel is all we hear.

---

6 Jeanette Robinson Murphy, "The Survival of African Music in America," in *The Negro and His Folklore in Nineteenth-Century Periodicals*, ed. Bruce Jackson (Austin, 1967), p. 329. This article originally appeared in *Popular Science Monthly*, LV (1899), 660–72.

7 Paul Laurence Dunbar, "An Ante-Bellum Sermon," in *Complete Poems* (New York, 1968), pp. 13–14.

8 William Wells Brown, *Clotel* (New York, 1969), p. 100.

But as soon as a slave begins to feel himself near a man, he wants a free gospel."[9]

The "free" or "whole gospel" of the slave usually emphasized God's imminent redemption of black Americans from slavery. At times God was seen as the exclusive agent of liberation, while at other times the militant agency of the blacks themselves was deemed essential. It is relatively easy to see how such a gospel differs from the somewhat practical affair endorsed by white Americans whose expanded enterprise, territorial acquisition, and institutional proliferation resulted in an ever-widening secularization of life. While white Americans expounded doctrines of progress and concerned themselves with what Herman Melville (in *Pierre*) called horological time, black Americans looked to an absolute, linear (chronometrical) time moving from the creation to the judgment day, which, they felt, would be the day of their liberation. White Americans, as R. W. B. Lewis, Perry Miller, and Leo Marx have demonstrated, considered themselves new Adams in a new Garden of Eden; they believed that thrift and industry, a powerful technology, the dictates of social Darwinism, and a laissez-faire economy would assure the endurance and growth of their paradise.[10] The black American's theological perspective, on the other hand, stressed his own "Egyptian captivity," not his ease in a new Eden. One result of these divergent views has been an opposition between the white and the black American's conceptions of the apocalypse.

Harold Simonson holds that it was only at the end of the nineteenth century (when Frederick Jackson Turner had announced the close of the frontier) that Americans *en masse* began to think and prophesy in ominous eschatological terms.[11] By contrast, such terms have always found significant place in the black American's vocabulary. The excoriation and diminution of white America has been viewed as a promise by black Americans almost from the beginning of their enslavement;

[9] Quoted from *Puttin' On Ole Massa*, ed. Gilbert Osofsky (New York, 1969), p. 35.

[10] R. W. B. Lewis, *The American Adam: Innocence, Tragedy, and Tradition in the Nineteenth Century* (Chicago, 1955); Perry Miller, *Errand into the Wilderness* (Cambridge, Mass., 1956); Leo Marx, *The Machine in the Garden: Technology and the Pastoral Ideal in America* (New York, 1967).

[11] Harold P. Simonson, *The Closed Frontier: Studies in American Literary Tragedy*, New York, 1970.

ich an event came to be considered a serious threat by the
majority of white Americans, however, only toward the close
f the nineteenth century. Harriet Beecher Stowe's *Uncle Tom's
Cabin*, Julia Ward Howe's "Battle Hymn of the Republic," the
writings of a number of the Garrisonian abolitionists, and Jack
London's *The Iron Heel* predict apocalyptic events that will
ead to a joyful liberation of the wretched of the earth. But the
one has generally been more sober when white American writers
have turned their attention to eschatological themes. Henry
Adams's *The Education of Henry Adams*, Nathaniel West's *The
Day of the Locust*, and William Styron's *Set This House on Fire*
ill depict apocalyptic events that bring about the ending of time,
ind the eschatological flames and energy destroy a Jerusalem
hat appears characteristically white—and American. The unknown folk bards and the conscious, creative artists of black
American culture, on the other hand, have turned to a discussion of the last acts and objects in a different mood, for blacks
have long believed that their dignity, status, and freedom as a
people are dependent upon the descent of an apocalypse on a
corrupt and oppressive white world, and a number of works in
the black American literary tradition give forceful expression
to this belief.

II

An early folk tale from the Gullah Islands off the coast of South
Carolina defines the terms of the black artist's concern with
apocalypse as a chastisement of the sinful oppressor. The tale
is entitled "Why Br'Gator's Hide Is So Horny," and the plot is
as follows.[12] Brer Rabbit is out walking one day when he comes
to the river, where he finds Brer Gator sunning himself. At this
time, Brer Gator's back was "smooth an' white as a catfish-skin,
so dat when he come out o' de water, an' lie down for sleep in
de sun-hot on de mud-bank, he shine like a piece o' silber." The
white, shining gator family was quite proud and felt that it was
far superior to all the land creatures.

12 *The Book of Negro Folklore*, ed. Langston Hughes and Arna Bontemps (New
York, 1969), pp. 23–30. The spirituals quoted in this essay also appear in this
work, pp. 279–311.

Brer Rabbit disturbed Brer Gator by asking after his family
The gator replied that everyone was just fine, couldn't be better.
Of course, he added, everything was expected to be fine for the
water creatures, and he just couldn't see how any creatures
could live on the land. This response piqued Brer Rabbit a
little, but he decided to remain calm, and replied: "Mebbe so.
We sho' is been seein' a heap o' trouble!" Brer Gator then asked
who trouble was; he said he didn't know trouble because he had
never seen him. Brer Rabbit couldn't believe what he heard,
since he knew the gator had just recently had some trouble with
the dog. The rabbit continued to play his role, seeing an opportunity in the gator's ignorance, and agreed to show him trouble
if the gator would meet him on the following Saturday.

Brer Gator was badgered by his wife and children into taking
the whole family along. Brer Rabbit was waiting for the gator
with his pipe in his mouth, and the journey to see trouble got
underway. When the group came to a large field of dry grass,
Brer Rabbit told the gators to wait for him because he heard
someone calling him. At the edge of the field, Brer Rabbit piled
up twigs and dry grass and dropped some of the coals from his
pipe into the pile. After a while, one of the gator children saw
fire approaching and shouted: "Look-a'-dere! . . . Mus' be dat
is Trouble." Brer Gator and Mrs. Gator agreed, and the family
judged trouble pretty until the sparks began to drop on their
backs. Jumping about and shouting, they rushed back to the
river. On the way, they passed Brer Rabbit who said: "Ki,
Br'Alligator! I reckin you is seen Trouble now! Git 'long back
in de water, where you belong. An' don't nebber, no mo', hunt
Trouble!" Brer Gator was too scorched to argue, and when he
and his family examined themselves a few days later, they found
that "de fire work on dem so bad dat dey white skin is just as
black an' crinkly as a burnt log o' wood, an' rough as a libe-oak
bark. Dat family done git swinged for bein' so fool. An' from
dat day to dis Gator hab a horny hide."

In this tale, the rabbit is never identified as black, but for the
southern agrarian folk (especially those on the Gullah Islands,
where isolation was almost total because whites could not en-
dure the climate) Brer Rabbit was a projection, a wish-fulfillment
figure who enacted the desires of the slave in tales the masters
deemed acceptable. The antagonist is clearly identified as white,

removed from Brer Rabbit and the other land creatures, and filled with a fateful hubris. Through cunning and trickery, the rabbit is able to bring about the chastisement of this oppressive figure; he provides the agency of a small apocalypse that surely delighted the slave narrator and the black listeners assembled to hear his tale. By contrast, the white American who encountered this same tale was likely to see it only as an amusing story for children. It is, of course, significant that the narrative's main character is the trickster. Even in the earliest folk art of the black American, the etiological animal tale, we find the expression of revolutionary social and religious concerns. The psychical identification of the slave with the trickster made it possible for the folk to depict apocalyptic events that would punish their white oppressors.

A more explicit statement of the connection between apocalypse and freedom is offered by David Walker's *Appeal; in Four Articles; Together with a Preamble, to the Coloured Citizens of the World, But in Particular, and Very Expressly, to Those of the United States of America* (1829). Walker was one of the first militant black abolitionists, and his book is one of the most revolutionary documents of the nineteenth century. Walker, however, seems a revolutionary more on the order of Oliver Cromwell than of Che Guevara. As did most abolitionists, Walker took God and the Bible as sanctions for his action, and he was not averse to prophesying a dire *eschat* for those whites who insisted on maintaining and defending the peculiar institution. In a note to the third edition of his work, he maintains that no nation has ever held its slaves in a state as "wretched, degraded and abject" as "the Americans (who are, notwithstanding, looking for the Millennial day) have us." The irony here is not only that white slaveholders are professing Christians, but also that they are naive anticipants of the judgment day. The final day, according to Walker, will bring nothing but pain and suffering to these white captors because the black people ("coloured citizens of the world") are God's chosen, and if God himself does not punish their oppressors, he will give blacks the authority to do so. The end of the old earth and the descent of the final destroying fires as depicted in the *Appeal* was an event that Walker thought all black men could look to with Christian joy and with a firm confidence that freedom would follow.

David Walker's primary role in the *Appeal* is that of abolitionist, and like other abolitionists (black and white), Walker
pointed out the inconsistencies of America's Christianity. Frederick Douglass did the same in the "Appendix" to the *Narrative
of the Life of Frederick Douglass, an American Slave, Written
by Himself*:

Dark and terrible as is this picture, I hold it to be strictly true of
the overwhelming mass of professed Christians in America. They
strain at a gnat, and swallow a camel. Could any thing be more true
of our churches? They would be shocked at the proposition of fel-
lowshipping a *sheep*-stealer; and at the same time they hug to their
communion a *man*-stealer, and brand me with being an infidel, if I
find fault with them for it.[13]

And commenting on the paradoxical nature of such terms as
"Christian slave-holders" and "democratic enslavers" in his
famous "Fourth of July Oration" (1852), Douglass foresaw the
possible destruction of the new American Eden:

Oh! be warned! be warned! a horrible reptile is coiled up in your
nation's bosom; the venemous creature is nursing at the tender breast
of your youthful republic; *for the love of God, tear away*, and fling
from you the hideous monster, and *let the weight of twenty millions,
crush and destroy it forever!*[14]

As the Civil War drew closer, Douglass, like most Americans,
grew increasingly pessimistic about the possibility of preserving
a paradisal harmony and union. And for many black Americans,
as Jeanette Robinson Murphy pointed out, the war itself was an
apocalypse sent from God through the agency of Abraham Lin-
coln, the abolitionists, and certain noted politicians such as
Charles Sumner and Thaddeus Stevens. Booker T. Washington
explains how the subliminal meanings of certain apocalyptic
folksongs surfaced as the time of liberation approached:

As the great day drew nearer, there was more singing in the slave
quarters than usual. It was bolder, had more ring, and lasted later
into the night. Most of the verses of the plantation songs had some
reference to freedom. True, they had sung those same verses before,

13 Frederick Douglass, *Narrative of the Life of Frederick Douglass, an American
Slave, Written by Himself* (New York, 1968), p. 123.
14 Quoted from *What Country Have I? Political Writings by Black Americans*,
ed. Herbert J. Storing (New York, 1970), p. 36.

but they had been careful to explain that the "freedom" in these songs referred to the next world, and had no connection with life in this world. Now they gradually threw off the mask; and were not afraid to let it be known that the "freedom" in their songs meant freedom of the body in this world.[15]

Washington's words lend point to the entire black American religious experience, for they necessitate a closer look at such seemingly otherworldly folk products as the spirituals and sermons. The spirituals were usually sung by a group, and in them God was generally viewed as the exclusive agent of the apocalypse, though in "Joshua Fit de Battle of Jericho," the overthrow of sinners is accomplished by an earthly agency. In black sermons, however, the preacher generally identifies himself as the person chosen by God to herald a fiery end of time that will come unless his listeners repent. In the *Appeal*, David Walker consummately assumes the preacher's role as a scolding, threatening, divinely-inspired herald of the apocalypse, and such a man is magnificiently described by James Weldon Johnson's "Listen, Lord—a Prayer":

> And now, O Lord, this man of God,
> Who breaks the bread of life this morning—
> Shadow him in the hollow of thy hand,
> And keep him out of the gunshot of the devil.
> Take him, Lord—this morning—
> Wash him with hyssop inside and out,
> Hang him up and drain him dry of sin.
> Pin his ear to the wisdom post,
> And make his words sledge hammers of truth—
> Beating on the iron heart of sin.
> Lord God, this morning—
> Put his eye to the telescope of eternity,
> And let him look upon the paper walls of time.
> Lord, turpentine his imagination,
> Put perpetual motion in his arms,
> Fill him full of the dynamite of thy power,
> Anoint him all over with the oil of thy salvation,
> And set his tongue on fire.[16]

15 Booker T. Washington, *Up from Slavery*, in *Three Negro Classics*, ed. John Hope Franklin (New York, 1969), p. 39.

16 James Weldon Johnson, *God's Trombones* (New York, 1969), p. 14. The work also includes seven folk sermons rendered in poetical form and literary English by Johnson.

Here is virtually a superman of salvation who resembles one
of the more memorable figures encountered in Revelation: "And
I saw another mighty angel come down from heaven, clothed
with a cloud: and a rainbow was upon his head, and his face
was as it were the sun, and his feet as pillars of fire."

The black preacher was viewed in apocalyptic terms for good
reason; one of the most familiar sermons delivered by black
ministers, according to Johnson, "began with the Creation, went
on to the fall of man, rambled through the trials and tribulations
of the Hebrew Children, came down to the redemption by
Christ, and ended with the Judgment Day and a warning and
an exhortation to sinners."[17] "The Wounds of Jesus," a sermon
from Zora Neale Hurston's *Jonah's Gourd Vine* (1934), ends
with stirring apocalyptic imagery and a call for repentance:

> He died for our sins.
> Wounded in the house of His friends.
> That's where I got off de damnation train
> And dat's where you must get off, ha!
> For in dat mor-ornin,' ha!
> When we shall all be delegates, ha!
> to dat Judgment Convention
> When de two trains of Time shall meet on de trestle
> And wreck de burning axles of de unformed ether
> And de mountains shall skip like lambs
> When Jesus shall place one foot on de neck of de sea, ha!
> One foot on dry land, ah
> When his chariot wheels shall be running hub-deep in fire
> He shall take His friends thru the open bosom of an
>   unclouded sky
> And place in their hands de "hosanna" fan
> And they shall stand 'round his beautific throne
> And praise His name forever, Amen.[18]

If we extend Washington's observations (and there is ample sub-
stantiation for his point of view in other narratives)[19] the reckon-

[17] *Ibid.*, p. 2.

[18] Bontemps and Hughes, *The Book of Negro Folklore*, p. 242. For other
examples of black folk preaching see William H. Pipes, *Say Amen, Brother!
Old-Time Negro Preaching: A Study in Frustration* (New York, 1951) and Bruce A.
Rosenberg, *The Art of the American Folk Preacher* (New York, 1970).

[19] Frederick Douglass, *Narrative*, pp. 31–32; and Gilbert Osofsky, *Puttin' On
Ole Massa*, pp. 30–35.

ng day and the joy promised by this sermon have a great deal to
do with a very temporal glory.

Black American spirituals offer further examples of the connection between apocalypse and freedom in black expression.
Taking the biblical story of Lazarus and Dives (Luke 16:19–31)
and combining it with the Genesis story of Noah, the black folk
composed "I Got a Home in Dat Rock":

> Rich man Dives, he lived so well,
> Don't you see?
> Rich man Dives, he lived so well,
> Don't you see?
> Rich man Dives, he lived so well,
> When he died he found a home in Hell,
> He had no home in dat rock,
> Don't you see?
>
> God gave Noah de Rainbow sign,
> Don't you see?
> God gave Noah de Rainbow sign,
> Don't you see?
> God gave Noah de Rainbow sign,
> No more water but fire next time,
> Better get a home in dat rock,
> Don't you see?

While the white American is not mentioned, Dives, the rich
man who refused Lazarus the crumbs from his table was more
than likely a symbolic projection of the enslavers. Taking the
role of the chosen people, the singers prophesy an apocalyptic
end to the world the slaveholders made. Spirituals such as "God's
Gonna Set Dis World on Fire," "Where Shall I Be When the
First Trumpet Sound," and "Joshua Fit the Battle of Jericho"
all threaten a terrible (often a flaming) end for sinners. The
singers, however, picture themselves in a safety perhaps to be
equated with freedom as the fire descends:

> I'm gonna drink that healin' water
> I'm gonna drink that healin' water,
> Some o' dese days . . . God knows it!
> I'm gonna drink that healin' water
> Some o' dese days.

Heretofore, we have dealt only with the folk art, the writings of abolitionists, and several works of the early twentieth century. The black man's conception of himself as one of the chosen people and his association of the idea of a fateful apocalypse with his acquisition of freedom can also be seen in the works of recent black American writers such as James Baldwin and LeRoi Jones. In the works of Baldwin and Jones, however, it is not the trickster, the abolitionist, the preacher, or a partial and omnipotent God who is responsible for the liberating destruction of the oppressor. Baldwin places great faith in the sensitive intellectual, while Jones champions the acts of the armed revolutionary.

The titles alone of works by Baldwin and Jones are enough to indicate they are concerned with apocalyptic themes. Baldwin called one volume *The Fire Next Time,* carrying us back to the spirituals, and Jones entitled an essay "The Last Days of the American Empire," echoing Gibbon's title and calling up visions of the final fires descending on the unjust of the earth.

Baldwin relates that Elijah Muhammad once asked him, "And what are you now?" He replied, "I'm a writer. I like doing things alone."[20] In effect, the writer for Baldwin takes the place of the abolitionist, the singer of the spirituals, and the preacher as the herald of apocalypse. It is necessary for men to listen to and act on his message if the final flames are not to roar through the land.

Essentially, Baldwin's message in *The Fire Next Time* and elsewhere is that the black American must accept his past as it is; he must acknowledge his history as one of slavery, brutality, and violence, but also of endurance. The black man cannot look to the East or to Africa for his past. Without looking back to a European innocence, the white American must also accept the past of his race for what it is—charged though it may be with blood guilt. If the white man acknowledges the humanity of the black and gives him his due, there is hope for the world. The black man, in turn, must give love. If individuals of both races don't act on the author's advice, there is no hope for the world. Destruction is inevitable, because man has now reached a point where he can exterminate himself with ease. As with the trickster tales, the spirituals, the sermons, the writings of the black abolitionists, and the works of James Weldon Johnson and Zora Neale Hur-

[20] James Baldwin, "Down at the Cross," in *The Fire Next Time* (New York, 1964), p. 97.

ston, Baldwin's essay sees the freedom of the black American as essential to the preservation of the world. The concluding lines of *The Fire Next Time* sum up his attitude:

I could also see that the intransigence and ignorance of the white world might make that vengeance inevitable—a vengeance that does not really depend on, and cannot really be executed by, any person or organization, and that cannot be prevented by any police force or army: historical vengeance, a cosmic vengeance, based on the law we recognize when we say, "Whatever goes up must come down." And here we are, at the center of the arc, trapped in the gaudiest, most valuable, and most improbable water wheel the world has ever seen. Everything now, we must assume, is in our hands; we have no right to assume otherwise. If we—and now I mean the relatively conscious whites and the relatively conscious blacks, who must like lovers, insist on, or create, the consciousness of the others—do not falter in our duty now, we may be able, handful that we are, to end the racial nightmare, and achieve our country, and change the history of the world. If we do not now dare everything, the fulfillment of that prophecy, recreated from the Bible in song by a slave, is upon us: *God gave Noah the rainbow sign, No more water, the fire next time!* (Pp. 140–41)

The words "Everything now, we must assume, is in our hands" echo ominously. Baldwin adopts a secular viewpoint and rests the total responsibility for the salvation of mankind in the hands of the sensitive individual, presumably talented artists and thinkers such as Baldwin himself. The writer, therefore, becomes a sort of agency and herald for the apocalypse, and it is worth noting that the writer for Baldwin is more a herald than a flamethrower. His talent is employed in bringing about the freedom of the black American with the threat (rather than the actual instigation) of an apocalyptic event.

Unlike Baldwin, LeRoi Jones, in "The Last Day of the American Empire," does not advocate love, nor does he think the apocalypse should be staved off. Jones would welcome the apocalypse as many slaves did the Civil War, considering it an eschatological and liberating experience. As a writer Jones casts himself in the role of herald and agent as well. The subtitle of Jones's essay is "Including Some Instructions for Black People," and this reveals Jones's position—he stands with those whom he describes as "standing on their porches with their rifles looking into a night made unfriendly by the hideousness of the white man's ego" (p.

205). Jones is against all of the "white eyes" and the MAWPs (Mad American White People). In his essay, he ruthlessly exposes the deceit and lies of the white oppressor, and the images he presents demonstrate the corruption of American society. James Bond, for example, though British, is a typical image of this society—the suave lover licensed to kill foreigners. Again, Amos Burke of the now defunct television series "Burke's Law" is also typical—the millionaire policeman who shows the clear connection between capitalism and police power.

Jones is an agent of apocalypse; he says he writes poems that are like bullets, and all of his work is dedicated to the destruction of white society and the creation of a new black Eden. The last lines of his essay give a clear statement of his policy:

I say if your hope is for the survival of this society, this filthy order, no good. You lose. The hope is that young blacks will remember all of their lives what they are seeing, what they are witness to just by being alive and black in America, and that eventually they will use this knowledge scientifically, and erupt like Mt. Vesuvius to crush in hot lava these willful maniacs who call themselves white Americans.[21]

As a revolutionary writer, Jones is the agent of an apocalypse that differs from any encountered so far in this discussion. The apocalypse is still one of fire, but it is to be brought about by the strong-willed black men whom Jones portrays so well in what he calls his photo-essay style.

III

The progression from "God's Gonna Set Dis World on Fire" to Jones's "The Last Day of the American Empire" not only illustrates that an exploration of recurrent philosophical themes offers a fertile approach to black American literature, but also demonstrates, once again, the unique character of the black experience. While whites were either ignoring threats to their New Jerusalem or—after the close of the frontier—bemoaning their impending doom, black Americans sang expectantly, preached inspiringly, and wrote passionately about the conflagration of a slave-holding society and about their subsequent emergence

[21] "The Last Days of the American Empire (Including Some Instructions for Black People)," in *Home* (New York, 1968), pp. 208-9.

from servitude. The agency of apocalypse depicted by the folk and by conscious, creative artists often reflects the degree of power held by black Americans at particular moments in their history. The trickster in "Why Br'Gator's Hide Is So Horny," for example, is one of the earliest heroes to bring about an apocalyptic event, and he is followed by the black abolitionist who helped to hasten the Civil War, which many blacks regarded as the fulfillment of God's covenant with Noah. And from the earliest days of slavery, preachers and singers of the spirituals have provided examples of the black American's belief in the apocalypse as a means to freedom. With the work of Baldwin and Jones, however, this theme takes a new and secularized form; the agency of apocalypse shifts to the writer and the armed revolutionary.

It seems clear that recent black writers have not been reluctant to follow the lead of Baldwin and Jones. Images of the fiery end of the world brought about or at least heralded by the revolutionary camp to which he grants his allegiance abound in the works of recent black writers. The bulk of the black population, now situated in the hearts of American cities, has shown its ability to ignite apocalyptic events during the past seven years, and black expression has chronicled this contemporary situation, making effective use of terms that grow out of the black American religious experience.

IV Revolution and Reform
Walker, Douglass, and the Road to Freedom

I

URING the first half of the nineteenth century, two monu
ments of the black literary tradition had their birth. One
was David Walker's *Appeal*, written in 1829, and the other
was Frederick Douglass's *Narrative of the Life of Frederick
Douglass, an American Slave, Written by Himself*, which ap
peared in 1845. Both captured the spirit of their epoch, and both
define certain modes, techniques, and conventions that since
their time have played significant roles in the literary tradition
of which they are a part.

The first half of the nineteenth century was one of the most
dynamic stages in American history. It was an age of territorial
expansion carrying the United States to the Pacific; new frontiers
were opening, and the quest for frontier was an important ele
ment in the American world view. The nation participated fully
in world trade, and its northern regions entered into the period
of growth that was eventually to carry America to the position of
the world's leading producer. It was an age in which power was
gradually diffusing itself and moving into the hands of the peo
ple, and the election of Andrew Jackson in 1828 and again in
1832 is perhaps the best manifestation of this diffusion of po
litical power.

To a certain extent early nineteenth-century America was like
early nineteenth-century England, where increasing industrial
ization brought about shifts in population and power. Like Eng
lishmen, Americans championed the idea of progress, and in an
age of expansion and shifting power, they looked toward a bright
and glorious future. England and America, moreover, were both
characterized by a high degree of evangelical zeal; belief in sal
vation by faith and grace and in the authority of the gospel found
many ardent followers.

Religious zeal, a moral impulse to reform, and utopian visions of the future—these three elements stand out in the history of England and America in the 1830s. In America they found their readiest expression in the abolitionist movement.[1] In England, the same impulses led to the abolition of West Indian slavery in 1833. William Lloyd Garrison, Wendell Phillips, Arthur Tappan, Charles G. Finney, and James Birney are the names most often associated with the American abolitionist movement. Garrison's *Liberator*, founded in 1831, was one of the many weeklies that aroused America's concern for the plight of the slave. Abolitionist newspapers provided a forum for free blacks in America, and until 1870 they were instrumental in focusing attention on essential reforms such as emancipation, free soil, women's rights, pacifism, and temperance.[2]

There were many reform movements in nineteenth-century America, but the abolitionist movement captured the imagination of a broad segment of the populace and seemed to express the spirit of the age. Numerous antislavery societies were established; by 1836 there were at least five hundred abolition societies in the free states, and by 1840 these societies had a membership of at least 150,000 persons.[3] The names on the membership rolls were not simply those of whites. As Benjamin Quarles has pointed out, "black Americans were conspicuously in their ranks from the outset."[4] Lerone Bennett also underscores the important role played by blacks in the movement: "In the forties, fugitive slaves moved into the front lines of the antislavery battle. No abolitionist meeting was complete without the presence of a Negro speaker or a Negro exhibit (a fugitive slave)."[5] Henry Highland Garnet, William Wells Brown, Robert Purvis, and Charles Redmond are just a few of the black Americans who made significant contributions.

[1] Richard O. Curry, ed., *The Abolitionists, Reformers or Fanatics?* (New York, 1965), p. 1.

[2] *The Anti-Slavery Standard, Pennsylvania Freeman, Anti-Slavery Bugle, Liberty Party Paper, North Star,* and *Frederick Douglass's Paper* were other influential newspapers that might well have adopted Garrison's motto: "I am in earnest—I will not equivocate—I will not excuse—I will not retreat a single inch—*and I will be heard.*"

[3] Curry, p. 2.

[4] Benjamin Quarles, *The Negro in the Making of America* (New York, 1968), p. 105.

[5] Lerone Bennett, *Before the Mayflower* (Baltimore, 1966), p. 137.

The zeal of the abolitionists led some to call them fanatics; others called them worse. The debate over their sanity, moreover, has yet to be resolved; Richard O. Curry's *The Abolitionists*, for example, is subtitled, "Reformers or Fanatics?" Allowing for prejudices and vested interests, it might be said that some abolitionists were more "engaged" than others: a distinction might be made between the "immediatists" who said "now" and meant this very moment and the temperate immediatists who endorsed reform rather than violent revolution. In both camps, however, religion was clearly the sanction for action, and "a merciful providence" had a great deal to do with how one proceeded. The polarity between revolution and reform in the abolitionist movement is well illustrated by the works of David Walker and Frederick Douglass. The Protestant ethical base of the abolitionist movement finds expression in the works of both writers.

II

David Walker was born free, and sometime before 1827 he left the South for Boston in order to escape an atmosphere of slavery and brutality. An observer and a traveller, Walker was so moved by what he had seen, read, and heard that he took pen in hand in 1829 and produced one of the most militantly revolutionary documents ever composed by a black American, *Appeal, in Four Articles; Together with a Preamble to the Coloured Citizens of the World, but in Particular, and Very Expressly to Those of the United States of America*. The prodigiousness of the title is more than matched by the volubility and anger of the text itself, for the book is virtually a cauldron of denunciation.

Walker assures us that all he reports proceeds from first-hand knowledge. At one point he says, "No man may think this book is made up of conjecture—I have travelled and observed nearly the whole of those things myself, and what little I did not get by my own observation, I received from those among the whites and blacks, in whom the greatest confidence may be placed."[6]

The *Appeal*, therefore, is a recounting of a man's life experiences and his emotional and intellectual reactions to it. On the basis of his own history, Walker sets out to prove that

[6] David Walker, *Appeal*, ed. Charles M. Wiltse (New York, 1969), p. 76.

. . . we Coloured People of these United States, are, the most
wretched, degraded and abject set of beings that ever lived since
the world began, down to the present day, and, that, the white Christians of America, who hold us in slavery, (or, more properly speaking,
pretenders to Christianity) treat us more cruel and barbarous than
any Heathen nation did any people whom it had subjected or reduced to the same condition, that the Americans (who are, notwithstanding, looking for the Millennial day) have us.[7]

Repeatedly, Walker draws on anecdotes and examples that he
has gathered during his travels or from his extensive knowledge
of conditions in the world at large—particularly in the "Southern
and Western States" of America, to which our attention is constantly directed in the *Appeal*. An incident, in which a group of
black slaves rebel against their black driver, killing his two white
assistants but allowing the driver to escape, leads Walker to a
series of bitter reflections on the consequences of the black man's
ignorance:

Here my brethren, I want you to notice particularly in the above
article, the *ignorant* and *deceitful actions* of this coloured woman.
I beg you to view it candidly, as for ETERNITY!!!! Here a *notorious
wretch*, with two other confederates had sixty of them in a gang,
driving them like *brutes*—the men all in chains and hand-cuffs, and
by the help of God they got their chains and hand-cuffs thrown off,
and caught two of the wretches and put them to death, and beat the
other until they thought he was dead, and left him for dead; however, he deceived them and rising from the ground, this *servile
woman* helped him upon his horse, and he made his escape. Brethren,
what do you think of this? Was it the natural *fine feelings* of this
woman, to save such a wretch alive? [P. 24]

The incident is taken from a Boston newspaper, but it becomes
much more than objective reportage in Walker's hands. He is
able to see all the implications of the event, and he reinforces
them by reference to his own experience (pp. 29–33). His encounters with a Negro bootblack, with a man who thinks his son
an accomplished scholar because he can write a neat hand, and
with black school children who make pretensions to learning
made him realize how deceived and wretched the black man is.
The bootblack feels that he will be happy so long as he has a good
trade; the proud father feels no regret that his son has none of

[7] Introductory Note to the third edition.

the "substance of learning"; and no one seems alarmed that "not more than one in thirty" of the black school children whom Walker examined in different parts of the country were able to answer questions on Murray's English Grammar.

Walker's examples lend immediacy to his *Appeal* and convince readers that they are not in the presence of a mere rhetorician. In his first article ("Our Wretchedness in Consequence of Slavery") Walker achieves the same effects by his use of world and scriptural history. Only a well-read man could use Joseph's plight in Egypt, the barbarity of the Turks, the Spartans' treatment of their Helots, and the condition of Roman slaves to prove that American slavery was one of the worst abuses humanity ever suffered. And in his third article ("Our Wretchedness in Consequence of the Preachers of the Religion of Jesus Christ"), Walker again shows his learning, citing scripture to demonstrate how white Europeans have perverted the dispensations of Christ (p. 35), tracing—with statistics—the development of slavery in America (p. 36), and illustrating the differences between Christianity's treatment of slaves and that accorded them by "Pagans, Jews, and Mahometans" (pp. 36–37). Walker's use of a variety of personal, historical, scriptural, and political examples gives the *Appeal* a convincing, firsthand quality.

In the process of indicting white Americans for their cruelty, Walker clearly wishes to emphasize certain ironies, especially the fact that in America the cruel enslavers were professing Christians, and that the enslavers wait, with eager expectations and hopes of reward, for the judgment day. He adopts many roles to prove his thesis, assuming many stances in the course of the *Appeal* in order to reinforce his proofs and point the way toward action.

One of Walker's most interesting roles (in addition to those of travelled observer and comparative historian) is that of the impassioned preacher, a scolding, chastising herald of apocalypse. We have seen this stance in black folklore (notably in the sermon "The Wounds of Jesus") and in the works of conscious literary artists such as James Weldon Johnson. At several points in the *Appeal* Walker identifies himself as one of God's messengers; in one instance he says of those who doubt his word:

Do they believe that I would be so foolish as to put out a book of this kind without strict—ah! very strict commandments of the Lord?

—Surely the blacks and whites must think that I am ignorant enough.
—Do they think that I would have the audacious wickedness to take
the name of my God in vain? [P. 71]

As a man commanded by God, Walker felt that it was his duty
to herald the apocalypse; throughout his text we see ominous
warnings of the impending doom of the American people:

In fact, they [white Americans] are so happy to keep in ignorance
and degradation, and to receive the homage and the labour of the
slaves, they forget that God rules in the armies of heaven and among
the inhabitants of the earth, having his ears continually open to
the cries, tears and groans of his oppressed people; and being a just
and holy Being will at one day appear fully in behalf of the oppressed,
and arrest the progress of the avaricious oppressors. . . . [P. 3]

But if they [whites] do not have enough to be frightened for yet, it
will be, because they can always keep us ignorant, and because God
approbates their cruelties, with which they have been for centuries
murdering us. The whites shall have enough of the blacks, yet, as true
as God sits on his throne in Heaven. [P. 32]

I know that thousands will doubt—they think they have us so well
secured in wretchedness, to them and their children, that it is impossible for such things to occur. So did the antideluvians doubt
Noah, until the day in which the flood came and swept them away.
So did the Sodomites doubt, until Lot had got out of the city, and
God rained down fire and brimstone from Heaven upon them, and
burnt them up. . . . So would Christian Americans doubt, if God
should send an Angel from Heaven to preach their funeral sermon.
The fact is, the Christians having a name to live, while they are dead,
think that God will screen them on that ground. [Pp. 72–73]

If there is to be an apocalypse, surely some chosen souls will be
saved; for Walker these are the "coloured" peoples of the world,
"for why should we be afraid, when God is and will continue, (if
we continue humble) to be on our side?" (p. 12). Later in the
Appeal, Walker shows that his people will not only be saved but
may well act as God's agents on earth:

But remember, Americans, that as miserable, wretched, degraded
and abject as you have made us in preceding, and in this generation,
to support you and your families, that some of you, (whites) on the
continent of America, will yet curse the day that you ever were born.
You want slaves, and want us for your slaves!!! My colour will yet,
root some of you out of the very face of the earth. [P. 72]

And he levels a scathing ultimatum, charged with emphatic rhetorical devices, at those who would doubt his warnings and proclamations: "Perhaps they will laugh at or make light of this; but I tell you Americans! that unless *you* speedily alter your course, *you* and your *Country are gone*!!!!!! For God Almighty will tear up the very face of the earth!!!" (p. 39). Like a true preacher, however, after citing an apocalyptic passage from Revelation, Walker suggests a way out for the enslavers:

Will the Lord suffer this people to go on much longer, taking his holy name in vain? Will he not stop them, preachers and all? O Americans! Americans! I call God—I call angels—I call men, to witness, that your Destruction *is at hand*, and will be speedily consummated unless you REPENT. [P. 43]

Walker thus views his message as the word of God revealed to an earthly herald, and like the preachers seen elsewhere in black expression, he acts like a man who has a good deal to do with the coming of the apocalypse, the salvation of the pure, and the condemnation of sinners.

Walker assumes at least two other roles in his *Appeal*. The first connects him with all that is considered highest in the American tradition; taking the stance of a radical in the manner of Thomas Paine, Nathan Hale, and Patrick Henry, he plays the role of the black founding father positing the conditions for the birth of freedom. We find him talking of the natural rights of the black American in his first article, and detailing how these rights have been "stolen" by the white oppressor. In the last article he deals with the plight of the black man in an exhaustive catalogue of brutalities inflicted by whites:

First, no trifling portion of them will beat us nearly to death, if they find us on our knees praying to God,—They hinder us from going to hear the word of God—they keep us sunk in ignorance, and will not let us learn to read the word of God, nor write—If they find us with a book of any description in our hand, they will beat us nearly to death—they are so afraid we will learn to read, and enlighten our dark and benighted minds—They will not suffer us to meet together to worship the God who made us. . . . [P. 65]

Walker goes on to list whipping, ear-cropping, branding, tongue-cutting, hand-cuffing, and brainwashing. Though the abuses are more cruel, the list serves the same function as the "long train of abuses" set forth in the Declaration of Independence. White America replaces George III as tyrant, and in particular, such prominent statesmen as Henry Clay and Thomas Jefferson himself. The irony is not complete, however, until Walker adopts a strategy that has been used recently by one of the more revolutionary black American organizations: he quotes from the Declaration of Independence and proceeds to ask rhetorical questions about the rights of the black American.

Walker clearly shows that the condition of the black American race is such that it can be justly labelled the victim of a long train of abuses and usurpations, and he affirms that the state of blacks is far worse than that of the American colonists at the end of the eighteenth century. If these conditions continue they, like the American colonists, will have no choice but to rise up, throw off their oppressors, and "provide new guards for their future security."

Walker goes to the same limits that the early radicals approached: the choice for him, as for Patrick Henry, was between liberty and death. When he threw down the gauntlet in print, he was aware that he was staking all:

I say, I do not only expect to be held up to the public as an ignorant, impudent and restless disturber of the public peace, by such avaricious Creatures, as well as a mover of insubordination— and perhaps put in prison or to death, for giving a superficial exposition of our miseries, and exposing tyrants. [P. 2]

At another point he says:

I therefore ask the whole American people, had I not rather die, or be put to death, than to be a slave to any tyrant, who takes not only my own, but my wife and children's lives by inches? Yea, would I meet death with avidity far! far! in preference to such *servile submission* to the murderous hands of tyrants. [P. 14]

And later in the *Appeal* he declares: "I write without the fear of man, I am writing for my God, and fear none but himself; they may put me to death if they choose—(I fear and esteem a good man however, let him be black or white)" (p. 54).

Walker's work, which differs from the somewhat sophisticated and aristocratic revolutionary fervor of a Patrick Henry, has an importance far beyond its reflection of an existing tradition. Walker's was a truly revolutionary consciousness, grounded not on reading and the consolations of philosophy, but on his personal experience as a black man in America. Lerone Bennett, who has appropriately called Walker the "nineteenth-century Fanon," feels that the *Appeal* marks an important stage in the black American's movement toward freedom: "The appearance of David Walker marked a transition in the liberation movement from the quiet protest of the colonial leaders to the revolutionary posture of the militant abolitionist."[8] And Charles Wiltse has said: "If any single event may be said to have triggered the Negro revolt, it is the publication of David Walker's *Appeal*. . . ."[9]

Walker's work is indeed a seminal and transitional one, for it stands at the beginning of an age of increased and fervent abolitionist agitation, opening the door into the active and ofttimes strident thirties. Walker is one of the first "John Brown" abolitionists, a man who believed in counterviolence as a means of checking violence:

. . . if you commence, make sure work—do not trifle, for they will not trifle with you—they want us for their slaves, and think nothing of murdering us in order to subject us to that wretched condition—therefore, if there is an *attempt* made by us, kill or be killed. [P. 25; Walker's emphasis]

In his first article, Walker praises the African general Hannibal for slaying the white Romans, and he goes on to demonstrate how the Haitian Revolution of 1791 offers a paradigm for black men all over the world. In Haiti, Toussaint L'Ouverture and his fellow black men overthrew the planter class and hacked and burned until they had secured their liberty, and Walker feels that the white tyrants received no more than they deserved. The American enslavers should receive the same treatment, he declares, "for we must remember that *humanity, kindness* and *the fear of the Lord*, does not consist in protecting devils" (p. 25). Later in the first article, Walker's advocacy of armed revolt becomes even clearer:

Now, I ask you, had you not rather be killed than to be a slave to a tyrant, who takes the life of your mother, wife and children, and

[8] Lerone Bennett, "The Fanon of the Nineteenth Century," in *Pioneers in Protest* (Chicago, 1968), p. 70.

[9] Charles M. Wiltse, Introduction to David Walker, *Appeal* (New York, 1969), p. vii.

answer God Almighty; and believe this, that it is no more harm for you to kill a man, who is trying to kill you, than it is for you to take a drink of water when thirsty; in fact, the man who will stand still and let another murder him, is worse than an infidel, and if he has common sense, ought not to be pitied. [Pp. 25–26]

Walker felt that his analysis of the black man's situation and his championing of violent rebellion were realistic, for "in some of the West-Indies Islands, and over a large part of South America, there are six or eight coloured persons for one white" (p. 63). Since the black men of the world have the numerical advantage, and since the treatment of blacks by whites leaves nothing in their hearts but "death alone" (p. 61), only ignorance and servility keep them from rising against their oppressors.[10]

Walker thus stands with the more militant abolitionists—with those who even today are labelled by some as "fanatics"—for his position was fervently bellicose. He spoke to the wretched of the earth as well as the enslavers, and he called for the immediate end of an oppressive institution. The existing fabric of society had to be changed instantly, and if the slitting of what he called "the devilish throat" of the oppressor from "ear to ear" was the only way, then Walker was for bringing out the sharp edges. He knew the danger of expounding such a philosophy—one that threatened the vested interests of the most powerful men in the country—and when he was found poisoned outside his second-hand clothes shop in Boston, "few doubted . . . that the most eloquent voice in the battle for Negro freedom had been violently stilled."[11] The spirit that Walker had set astir, however, was not to be denied. It was too much in keeping with the moral

---

[10] This is the reason that an entire article of the *Appeal* is devoted to "Our Wretchedness in Consequence of Ignorance"; education, according to Walker, is a necessary step in the process of liberation. What he has in mind is not just a simple grasp of the fundamentals of reading and writing, but "the substance of learning." He feels that it is the duty of all black men of "common sense" to work at educating their ignorant brothers, who must be taught that their interests do not lie with the oppressors. They must learn, he feels, that any act of treachery or deceit (the offspring of ignorance) militates against their own humanity, and that true learning leads to astute perception, useful work, and a liberation of the human spirit. Education of ignorant blacks will lead, Walker avers, to the "*entire emancipation of your enslaved brethren all over the world*" (p. 29). Walker's ideas on education anticipate not only those of W. E. B. Du Bois as set forth in *The Souls of Black Folk*, but also the philosophy behind today's liberation schools.

[11] Wiltse, p. xi.

fervor, the demand for immediate freedom, and the call for the repentance of the sinful that characterized its age to be denied.

III

One aspect of the *Appeal* that calls attention to itself is the author's style; Walker takes pains to make each page a searing statement of the "condition of America." In the *Appeal*, therefore, we see the use of such devices as repetition, exclamation, and sudden breaks in thought, as well as italics and bizarre punctuation—all of which reflect strong emotion and serve to convey emphasis:

> This country is as much ours as it is the whites, whether they will admit it now or not, they will see and believe it by and by. They tell us about prejudice—what have we to do with it? Their prejudices will be obliged to fall like lightning to the ground, in succeeding generations; not, however, with the will and consent of all the whites, for some will be obliged to hold on to the old adage, viz: the blacks are not men, but were made to be an inheritance to us and our children for ever!!!!!! I hope the residue of the coloured people, will stand still and see the salvation of God and the miracle which he will work for our delivery from wretchedness under the Christians!!!!!! [Pp. 56–57]

Within this brief passage, Walker deals with four different points, and it is the sheer force of the statement that holds all together. First there is the assertion of the black man's right to America, which is the essential point, but this veers by association into a brief reflection on prejudice, which in turn leads to a reference to the assumed inferiority of the black man. Finally, we move entirely away from the main point as Walker threatens the country with God's vengeance and drives home once again the irony of Christian enslavers. There is neither analysis nor description, only declamation and assertion. Throughout the *Appeal* such passages occur at the end of lengthy discussions of the condition of the "coloured people of the world," passages that are more effective for the fire and fervor they inspire than for the knowledge they contain or the subtlety they display.

Walker's style is in perfect harmony with the tone and intent of his *Appeal*, for the title alone tells us that the author will attempt to evoke the strongest response possible, and in the text he ranges from oracular denunciation, to sarcasm, to lamentation. The nearest parallel to this aspect of Walker's work would be, perhaps, the words of the Old Testament prophets, who were never averse to sounding their messages in organ tones, or taking the Lord God Almighty as sanction for their actions. There are, however, New Testament parallels in the *Appeal*, for Walker's four articles are similar to the Pauline Epistles. Each article begins with a didactic statement addressed either to "My Beloved brethren," or "my brethren," and goes on to point out what course God and common sense dictate for the black man. Thus "Article II" opens poetically with the words: "Ignorance, my brethren, is a mist, low down into the very dark and almost impenetrable abyss in which our fathers for many centuries have been plunged." The article goes on to expound the effects of ignorance on the black man and the means by which he can rise from the misty abyss. But the slight formal parallel with the Pauline Epistles does not conceal the fact that Walker's message is fundamentally governed by the old dispensation: the law of the *Appeal* is "an eye for an eye." It is obvious that the author's purpose is to bring about the redemption of his people and herald the divine wrath that will beset their sinful oppressors.

Walker's fiery style also finds parallel within the black American literary tradition, for his tone and technique are much like those of early declamatory poets such as Jupiter Hammon, George Moses Horton, and Frances E. W. Harper. Characterizing the verse of these writers in *Early Black American Poets*, William Robinson says:

These lines were usually most effective when they were read aloud, or, more accurately, when they were "rendered" on platforms of convention halls or opera houses or church pulpits across the country; sometimes freely participated in by audience responses, laughter, applause, these lines were close to the sermons.[12]

Walker's style is enriched by all the vividness and energy of the black oral tradition. In Frances Harper's "The Slave Auction" and John Jasper's famous sermon, "De Sun Do Move," one

---

[12] William H. Robinson, Jr., ed., *Early Black American Poets* (Dubuque, Iowa, 1969), pp. xv–xvi.

can observe how close the *Appeal* is to oral literature. Mrs. Harper begins:

> The sale began—young girls were there,
>   Defenceless in their wretchedness,
> Whose stifled sobs of deep despair
>   Revealed their anguish and distress.
> And mothers stood with streaming eyes,
>   And saw their dearest children sold;
> Unheeded rose their bitter cries,
>   While tyrants bartered them for gold.

Jasper, toward the end of his sermon, addresses his congregation:

Is I got you satisfied yet? Has I proven my point? Oh, ye whose hearts is full of unbelief! Is you still holding out? I reckon de reason you say de sun don't move is cause you are so hard to move your self. You is a real trial to me, but, never mind, I ain't given you up yet and never will. Truth is mighty; it can break de heart of stone and I must fire another arrow of truth out of de quiver of de Lord.[13]

Striking imagery, pictures of despair, and weighted, emotion-charged phrases ("tyrants bartered them for gold")—all of these are found in Jasper and Harper; they are almost essential components of a tradition that addresses itself to the "coloured people of the world" on the theme of freedom. Walker even uses some of the same images. He constantly points to the avariciousness of the whites, and the phrase "dig up gold and silver for them" is repeated again and again. Like Jasper, Walker is capable of moving from the most colloquial analogy—"There are indeed, more ways to kill a dog, besides choking it to death with butter" (p. 13)—to the most elaborate metaphor. Speaking of the supposed inferiority of blacks to whites, as asserted by Thomas Jefferson, he says: "I do not know what to compare it to, unless, like putting one wild deer in an iron cage, where it will be secured, and hold another by the side of the same, then let it go, and expect the one in the cage to run as fast as the one at liberty" (p. 10). In this instance, Walker makes effective use of animal imagery, another feature of the black folk tradition. Attacking the chattel principle of American slavery, he talks of blacks being treated as if they were brutes—rattlesnakes, bulls,

[13] *The Book of Negro Folklore*, ed. Arna Bontemps and Langston Hughes (New York, 1958), p. 230.

hogs, and horses; speaking of the ferocity of black men engaged in rebellion, he describes enraged lions and tigers.

Like the black folk sermons that came before and the black declamatory poetry that was contemporary with it, David Walker's *Appeal* is a direct, emotional plea which attempts to capture in written form the force of black oratory—its imagery, rhythm, intonation, and diction. Its style is anything but calm and sophisticated. Walker was determined to convey his beliefs to others by any means he could command; that this was often done at the expense of the "literary" values does not seem to have mattered. If emotional response is a fit criterion for determining the success of an author's attempt to instill in us an ideology, however, Walker must receive a positive evaluation; one cannot help being stirred by the *Appeal*.

Matters are quite different when we turn to Frederick Douglass's *Narrative*. The work begins, in the manner of so many slave narratives, at the lowest ebb of humanity; the narrator does not know his age or his father's identity. As nearly as he can ascertain, his father was a white man—his master. He thus belongs to the class of the "tragic mulatto," a figure used by abolitionist writers to symbolize the displacement of the black American caught between two worlds as well as the master's miscegenatory desires. He tells us that he was never close to his mother, since he saw her only four or five times before she died. This is not to say that Douglass starts by presenting himself as an oppressively tragic figure; on the contrary, one is immediately impressed by the straightforward, unornamented presentation with which the *Narrative* opens. Douglass simply says: "I was born in Tuckahoe, near Hillsborough, and about twelve miles from Easton, in Talbot County, Maryland."[14] This approach, much like Walker's, is as detailed and realistic an account as one could imagine. From the beginning, however, we receive more than simple narration; we are plunged at once into an agrarian environment with the narrator's dry quip about the slave and the horse who are in the same condition since neither knows his age. The agrarian setting is further established by the enumeration of the seasons of the slave's year: "planting-time," "harvest-time," "cherry-time," "spring-time," and "fall-time."

---

[14] *Narrative of the Life of Frederick Douglass* (New York, 1968), p. 21.

Douglass's concern with a realistic setting and straightforward narration (as opposed to Walker's flights of rhetoric) results in part from Douglass's almost exclusive attention to the temporal. Walker, who often wrote in prophetic tones of God's revelations, was never averse to moving in divine regions. For Douglass, however, religion was a much more practical affair. He views Christianity as "pure, peaceable, and impartial" (p. 120), as did the evangelical upper middle-class of nineteenth-century England and America. Although in the "Appendix" to the *Narrative* he turns a scorn equal to Walker's on the "slaveholding religion" of America, he very seldom addresses his audience in the tone of the fire-and-brimstone preachers of America's late-eighteenth-century religious revivals. In the *Narrative* he always seems to view religion as a pursuit designed to make men better and more dignified while on earth; the example of Jesus Christ offers him a paradigm for emulation, while for Walker it was a celestial threat to be used against the sinful and the skeptical. Douglass takes "the Christianity of Christ" (in its most incarnate form) as a sanction for his actions, and proceeds on a much more mundane level than his contemporary.

The techniques that we encounter on the first page of Douglass's work, therefore—the stark, visualized narration and the dry, ironic wit, the versimilitude, and the agrarian setting—continue throughout the *Narrative*; they make the work at once simple and enthralling. Douglass is far removed from the impassioned writer of the *Appeal*, but interestingly enough his work brings home its point just as effectively as Walker's. Perhaps the difference between the two resides in the fact that Douglass was at the beginning of a long and fruitful career when he wrote his *Narrative*; Walker, on the other hand, was an embittered middle-aged man, screaming, as a last, desperate measure, at the "world's wrong." Douglass, moreover, was born with a different gift of words, an ability to transport audiences, as Bennett has pointed out, "to slave row," by his highly artistic and sophisticated use of language. While Walker tried to bring about changes by explosive words, cascading phrases, and pyrotechnic catalogues, Douglass was content to present a bleak picture in a sparse style and the economy of his style tends to reinforce the poverty and oppressiveness of the situations which he describes. Here, for example, is his description of a whipping:

Before he commenced whipping Aunt Hester, he took her into the kitchen, and stripped her from neck to waist, leaving her neck, shoulders, and back, entirely naked. He then told her to cross her hands, calling her at the same time a d---d b---h. After crossing her hands, he tied them with a strong rope, and led her to a stool under a large hook in the joist, put in for the purpose. He made her get upon the stool, and tied her hands to the hook. [Pp. 25–26]

The passage continues in this manner, and the details are so specific and the tone so matter-of-fact that we are almost lulled into insensitivity. We awake with a start when we recall what is actually going on, and the impression that Douglass's presentation of human cruelty makes is a lasting one.

The impact of Douglass's straightforward narration is again demonstrated in his account of the murder of a slave for disobedience:

The first call was given. Demby made no response, but stood his ground. The second and third calls were given with the same result. Mr. Gore then, without consultation or deliberation with any one, not even giving Demby an additional call, raised his musket to his face, taking deadly aim at his standing victim, and in an instant poor Demby was no more. His mangled body sank out of sight, and blood and brains marked the water where he had stood. [P. 40]

Daniel Defoe or Victor Hugo might well have been proud of this description. The only hints of the author's bias are the words *poor* and *victim*, but with the help of these two words in the proper places, Douglass is able to present a scene of almost unimaginable brutality. A final example further reveals Douglass's craftsmanship; he describes his reduction to a state of abject servility at the hands of a slave breaker: "I was broken in body, soul, and spirit. My natural elasticity was crushed, my intellect languished, the disposition to read departed, the cheerful spark that lingered about my eye died; the dark night of slavery closed in upon me; and behold a man transformed into a brute!" (p. 75). A more telling account of the fall into the slough of despond could hardly be given; the passage is not high-flown, it is not allegorical, it is not symbolic; it is a simple account of the effects of slavery.

Douglass was a masterful chronicler of horrors, but to present him solely in this light is to misrepresent his work. The *Narra-*

tive is charged with a subtle, dry, and ironic humor, which provides comic relief and adds to the reader's sense of a detached and objective narrator. Commenting on the increase of mulatto children in the South, Douglass remarks:

If the lineal descendents of Ham are alone to be scripturally enslaved, it is certain that slavery at the south must soon become unscriptural; for thousands are ushered into the world, annually, who, like myself, owe their existence to white fathers, and those fathers most frequently their own masters. [P. 24]

Of the demise of a particularly cruel overseer, Douglass says: "His death was regarded by the slaves as the result of a merciful providence" (p. 30). Noting the frequent controversies among slaves as to which had the wealthiest master, he comments:

These quarrels would almost always end in a fight between the parties, and those that whipped were supposed to have gained the point at issue. They seemed to think that the greatness of their masters was transferable to themselves. It was considered as being bad enough to be a slave; but to be a poor man's slave was deemed a disgrace indeed! [P. 37]

Douglass's humor is valuable not simply because it gives us relief from the gruelling details of slavery. It brings us close to the essential humanity of the situation, and more important, it leads us to a balanced and realistic point of view, for if it is a humor of detached irony, it is also, like Wordsworth's, one of loving kindness. Douglass does not turn a satirical, objective glance on the follies of mankind; his smile, like that of Richard Wright's protagonist in *Native Son*, is "a faint, wry, bitter smile." While fully aware of the ridiculousness of certain human situations, he also realizes his own involvement in them and their larger implications.

While humor adds a degree of realism to the *Narrative*, it is Douglass's verisimilitude that brings us fully in touch with the experiences of the man behind the work. We are placed directly on the scene by the author's close attention to specific detail. We learn, for example, the exact number of Colonel Lloyd's slaves, horses, and cultivated acres. We become acquainted with the narrator's place of residence in Baltimore in terms of the area, the street, the neighbors, and the treatment accorded the neighbors' slaves. We learn exactly how wheat was fanned in Douglass's day, how many men it took to do the job, and the assignment of each.

Douglass's skill at characterization and his ability to evoke a particular setting also lend an air of reality to the *Narrative.* Nearly every activity and character we encounter is connected with an agrarian scene. We watch harvesting and the transporting of goods by water; we witness the actions of overseers, Southern preachers, and slave breakers; we see the slave cabins, barns, and stables. There is no hothouse atmosphere in Douglass's work; never is life reduced to the taking of toast and tea. The world of the *Narrative* is a world of action, one in which only the strong and determined survive. Moreover, Douglass is able to populate his world with highly individualized and believable characters—Captain Auld, Mr. Covey, and Mr. Freeland, for example. The narrator's powers of characterization may be seen in his description of Captain Auld:

His airs, words, and actions, were the airs, words, and actions of born slaveholders, and, being assumed, were awkward enough. He was not even a good imitator. He possessed all the disposition to deceive, but wanted the power. Having no resources within himself, he was compelled to be the coypist of many, and being such, he was forever the victim of inconsistency; and of consequence he was an object of contempt, and was held as such even by his slaves. [Pp. 66–67]

Douglass demonstrates in this passage one of his favorite techniques—the use of antithesis.

One can scarcely treat the agragrian settings and characters in Douglass's *Narrative* without some discussion of the animal metaphors that appear in most of the chapters of the *Narrative.* We have already noted the quip about the horse who does not know his age; and Douglass uses a similar figure to describe his joy when given the chance to go to Baltimore: "It was almost a sufficient motive, not only to make me take off what would be called by pig-drovers the mange, but the skin itself" (p. 44). Speaking of the anguish that resulted from a grasp of his situation, Douglass comments: "In moments of agony, I envied my fellow-slaves for their stupidity. I have often wished myself a beast. I preferred the condition of the meanest reptile" (p. 55). These images, of course, serve to reinforce Douglass's descriptions of the "soul-

killing" effects of slavery; in a word, they make the effects of the
three-fifths clause immediate. Slaves, like horses and other wild
animals, were "broken." Like Walker, Douglass is aware of
American slavery's chattel principle, which equated slaves with
livestock, and he is not reluctant to employ animal metaphors
to capture the general inhumanity of the system. Moreover, as
were the slave narrators of black animal tales, he was surely aware
that he and his "loved fellow-slaves" were usually on better terms
with the animals than with the owners of the farms and plantations on which they worked.

Douglass's work is a chronicle of the "soul-killing" effect slavery had on both master and the slave. Time and again in the
Narrative men's hopes for a better life are crushed: humans are
whipped and slaughtered like animals; men and women are
changed into maniacal and sadistic creatures by power; the
strength of mind and body is destroyed by an avaricious and degrading system. Captain Auld, Douglass and his fellow slaves,
Mrs. Hugh Auld, Mr. Covey, Anthony Auld—practically every
character we encounter in the *Narrative* is rendered less human
by the effects of slavery. Douglass's work, however, does not
simply describe the degradation occasioned by slavery; it also
illustrates how a sense of community, a spirit of revolt and resistance, and a mastery of disguise and deportment—black survival values which we encountered in the folk tradition—assist
in the development and ultimate escape of the person who is
willing to employ them. We are confronted in the *Narrative* with
a record of the early development of one individual, a *Bildungs-
roman*, which records the growth to manhood of a small slave
boy whom we first see in a tow-linen shirt enjoying a relatively
work-free life. Then we see a boy at twelve years of age playing
the trickster in order to acquire the rudiments of education:

After that, when I met with any boy who I knew could write, I
would tell him I could write as well as he. The next word would be,
"I don't believe you. Let me see you try it." I would then make the
letters which I had been so fortunate as to learn, and ask him to beat
that. In this way I got a good many lessons in writing, which it is
quite possible I should never have gotten in any other way. [Pp.
57–58]

At sixteen the boy adopts the code of the badman hero and
wrestles a fierce slave breaker into submission, vowing after the

struggle that "the white man who expected to succeed in whipping, must also succeed in killing me" (p. 83). The nineteen-
year-old *man*, with his fellow slaves, makes an abortive attempt
for freedom, and the twenty-year-old man finally gains his liberty
using the same type of disguise and deportment that we see in
"The Watcher Blinded."[15] Douglass does not tell us so in the
Narrative, but he made his escape to the North by wearing a
sailor's uniform and travelling as a free man.

We must admit that at times the author grows maudlin (in
describing the plight of his grandmother, for example), and at
times he is clearly too rhetorical (the soliloquy by the bay). For
the most part, however, he is a candid, witty and thorough narrator, able to play the diverse stops of the human condition with
consummate skill. It seems appropriate, therefore, to classify the
Narrative as a consciously literary work, and one of the first
order. The black folk background manifests itself in the values
that make survival possible in a brutal system, as well as in individual incidents, such as that in which Sandy Jenkins gives Douglass a root for his protection:

> He told me, with great solemnity, I must go back to Covey; but that
> before I went, I must go with him into another part of the woods,
> where there was a certain *root*, which, if I would take some of it with
> me, carrying it *always on my right side*, would render it impossible
> for Mr. Covey, or any other white man, to whip me. [P. 80]

Douglass, like thousands of his fellow black men, attributes some
power to the root even though he knew (at the time he was writing his *Narrative*) that his own strength and spirit of resistance
had perhaps more to do with his escaping Covey's intended lash-
ing than anything else. He again employs and helps to define folk
tradition when he deals with the songs of his fellow slaves. He
notes that the songs had a subliminal or hidden component:
"They would sing [the songs] as a chorus, to words which to
many would seem unmeaning jargon, but which, nevertheless,
were full of meaning to themselves" (p. 31). He goes on to show
that they were actually sorrow songs—"Slaves sing most when
they are most unhappy"—and adds: "To those songs I trace my
first glimmering conception of the dehumanizing character of
slavery" (p. 32). What we have, then, is both explication and ap-

---

15 Bontemps and Hughes, p. 9.

preciation of the folk heritage. Finally, Douglass turns a deflating irony on white preachers. Of Reverend Rigby Hopkins, a devout religionist, he says:

Mr. Hopkins was even worse than Mr. Weeden. His chief boast was his ability to manage slaves. The peculiar feature of his government was that of whipping slaves in advance of deserving it. He always managed to have one or more of his slaves to whip every Monday morning. He did this to alarm their fears, and strike terror into those who escaped. [P. 87]

The hypocrisy and pretension here are similar in some respects to the human failings seen in black preacher tales, though the purpose of the narration in this instance is much more serious.

Although the connection of Douglass's work with the black American folk tradition is clear, his obvious concern for the craft of writing places the *Narrative* in the realm of sophisticated literary autobiography. More specifically, Douglass's work is a spiritual autobiography akin to the writings of such noted white American authors as Cotton Mather, Benjamin Franklin, and Henry Adams. The narrator wishes to set before the reader not only his fully realized spiritual self, but also the hallowed values that made possible such a self. The *Narrative*, however, can be distinguished from the works of white American spiritual autobiographers because its essential goal is physical freedom. The narrator is not seeking to become one among the divine elect, nor is he attempting to forge a private, moralizing self as a foil to an intensely practical and political age that stressed the virtues of the public man. He seeks to move, by any means necessary, from a cruel physical bondage to freedom. Arna Bontemps is correct, therefore, in designating Douglass's *Narrative* a representative work in a separate American genre—the slave narrative.[16] The unique angle of vision that characterizes Douglass's work is—for obvious reasons—unmatched in the white American autobiographical tradition, and the author's handling of this perspective is among the most accomplished efforts in the tradition of black autobiography. And his achievements in this genre place him in the front ranks of black authors, since the autobiographical mode is one of the most important in the black Ameri-

16 Arna Bontemps, ed., *Great Slave Narratives* (Boston, 1969), p. xvii.

:an literary tradition. The tasks of portraying the unique character of one's group and of selectively recovering the self, which
many writers have considered distinct, are one for the black autobiographer. Douglass's narrator not only secures his own liberty,
but also becomes something of a mythic figure, taking his place
in the same framework that includes the drinking gourd, the un-
derground railroad, and the North Star.

IV

Although an orator himself, Frederick Douglass, unlike David
Walker, was not interested in rendering the intonation and diction of oratory into written form. While the latter's work parallels that of the declamatory poets of black America, Douglass is
allied with the formalists. William Robinson characterizes the
formalist poets (Phillis Wheatley, George M'Clellan, Ann Plato,
and Henrietta Cordelia Ray) as those who "reveal formal influences of classical propriety and restraint and conscious control. . . ."[17] Douglass effectively applies sophisticated literary
techniques—irony, wit, caricature, understatement, humor; he
never lacks the right word or the proper anecdote to emphasize
his point; and he relies upon masterful and convincing literary
presentation rather than fiery rhetoric. In fact, it is the passages
in which he lapses into oratory that detract from the overall effect of his work. The differences in the forms and styles employed by Douglass and Walker bespeak a larger difference, for
David Walker was, in essence, a nineteenth-century revolutionary, and Douglass was a reformer. The *Appeal* reflects the
values of those who are labelled "fanatics," while the *Narrative
of the Life of Frederick Douglass* manifests the values of the Garrisonian abolitionist reformers who were in favor of moral sua-
sion and opposed to any interaction (especially that of a political
character) with slaveholders.

Walker's work, addressed to the "coloured people of the
world," is an impassioned, ofttimes bitter appeal for revolutionary action. Douglass's is one of the most finished of many slave
narratives, which generally were written for abolitionist purposes

17 Robinson, p. xvi.

and principally for white readership. The incentive for this work was provided by reports that many whites in the audiences Douglass addressed under the auspices of the *Massachusetts Anti-Slavery Society* could not believe such polished speeches came from a man who had been a slave. Philip Foner writes:

Douglass was aware that if such reports continued, they would be fatal to his effectiveness as an Abolitionist agent. So he resolved to throw caution to the winds and write the story of his life. During the winter months of 1844–45 he was busily engaged in setting down an account of his slave experiences.[18]

Douglass intended to convince his white readers that he had suffered the dire effects of slavery, presumably hoping that in their moral outrage they would first acknowledge his remarkable achievement and then go forth to protest the abuses of slavery in America. The prime motivating force for his work and his Garrisonian stance help to explain his restrained posture and sophisticated style.

In some ways these same factors distinguish Douglass's work from the poorer slave narratives. In his attempts to persuade and convince, the author was forced to go beyond the format that was later to become standard for the slave chronicle. We are confronted with a host of fully rounded characters in the *Narrative*; we have a number of finely drawn scenes presented one after the other; and while we sense the irony, we also sense the genuine feeling of sincerity in the work. Only a few American narratives have such characteristics, and only one by an African is so distinguished. (The narratives of Solomon Northup and Henry Bibb are on a par with Douglass's; William Wells Brown's, which copies incidents from Douglass's, has little of the force and power of the latter's; and Gustavus Vassa's *The Life of Olaudah Equiano or Gustavus Vassa the African* is the only close parallel written by an African slave.) Douglass provided one of the most popular and enthralling works of literature written in the nineteenth century and, ironically, he intentionally produced it for an audience almost exclusively white.

Audience expectations, if taken alone, are enough to account for the aesthetic differences in the *Narrative* and the *Appeal*, but

[18] Philip S. Foner, *Frederick Douglass* (New York, 1969), p. 59.

beyond these differences there are significant ideological ones. Douglass worked within the existing order to obtain his most salient victories: he was editor and publisher of the *North Star, Frederick Douglass's Paper,* and *The New National Era;* he worked throughout much of his life as an abolitionist or reform lecturer; he served as marshal of the United States for the District of Columbia; and he was minister-resident and consul-general to the Republic of Haiti. Walker, on the other hand, wrote for two black abolitionist newspapers—*Freedom's Journal* and *Rights of All*—and was a seller of secondhand clothes whose entire life, as far as we know, was devoted to promulgating a violent overthrow of the existing order. He placed copies of his *Appeal* in the pockets of the clothes which he sold to seamen who were likely to make their way to the South, and he devoted his last energies to revising and editing the third edition of the *Appeal,* one of the most revolutionary texts produced in the nineteenth century. Not that Douglass, who helped to desegregate the public schools of Rochester, New York[19] and talked of striking the "first blow," did not take decisive actions. The dichotomy in approach is somewhat like that between the doctrines of the late Martin Luther King and those of Eldridge Cleaver and Bobby Seale. At times Douglass spoke more forcefully than Dr. King ever did; he often mentioned "blows," "bullets," and "the cartridge box," and he was in great sympathy with John Brown's plan to establish a garrison of runaway slaves in the Allegheny Mountains[20]—although shortly before the raid on Harper's Ferry, he refused to join Brown's party.[21]

Given their significant ideological differences, it is not surprising that Douglass's *Narrative* is akin in style and sensibility to Ralph Ellison's *Invisible Man* and James Baldwin's *Go Tell It on the Mountain,* while Walker's *Appeal* is closer to Eldridge Cleaver's *Soul on Ice.* In one of his fine autobiographical moments, Baldwin describes John Grimes's descent into the white world of New York: "These glories were unimaginable—but the city was real. He stood for a moment on the melting snow, distracted, and then began to run down the hill, feeling himself fly

19 *Ibid.,* pp. 127–29.
20 *Ibid.,* pp. 174–75.
21 Bennett, *Pioneers in Protest,* p. 201.

as the descent became more rapid, and thinking: 'I can climb back up. If it's wrong, I can always climb back up.' "[22] And in *Invisible Man*, Ellison's autobiographical narrator describes a scene in the chapel of a black Southern college:

Here upon this stage the black rite of Horatio Alger was performed to God's own acting script, with millionaires come down to portray themselves; not merely acting out the myth of their goodness, and wealth and success and power and benevolence and authority in cardboard masks, but themselves, these virtues concretely. Not the wafer and the wine, but the flesh and the blood, vibrant and alive, and vibrant even when stooped, ancient and withered. (And who, in the face of this, would not believe? Could even doubt?)[23]

The autobiographical impulse is present in the novels of both Baldwin and Ellison, and it is the informing principle of Douglass's work. The uncertainty of Baldwin's John Grimes as he races toward one type of freedom is much like that of Douglass and his friends as they plan their escape in the *Narrative*; and the combination of irony with the amazing force of description in Ellison's passage is reminiscent of the wit and energy that exposes pretenders throughout the *Narrative*. The finish of style, descriptive power, and ease of narration seen in Baldwin and Ellison as they move their protagonists from bondage toward freedom find ready parallel in Douglass's work.

A passage from *Soul On Ice* demonstrates how close the work as a whole is to Walker's *Appeal*, and how far removed both are from the best of Douglass, Baldwin, and Ellison. Speaking of Muhammad Ali, Cleaver writes:

A racist Black Muslim heavyweight champion is a bitter pill for racist white America to swallow. Swallow it—or throw the whole bit up, and hope that in the convulsions of your guts, America, you can vomit out the poisons of hate which have led you to a dead end in this valley of the shadow of death.[24]

There is a distinct affinity between this address to the country at large, ringing with denunciation and black pride, and any number of passages in Walker's *Appeal*. In essence, the difference between Douglass, Baldwin, and Ellison on one hand and

---

[22] James Baldwin, *Go Tell It on the Mountain* (New York, 1963), p. 31.

[23] Ralph Ellison, *Invisible Man* (New York, 1952), p. 101.

[24] Eldridge Cleaver, *Soul on Ice* (New York, 1968), p. 96.

Walker and Cleaver on the other is the difference between the self-conscious, controlled literary artist and the impassioned pamphleteer. This is by no means to say that the latter two never transcend the limits of the pamphleteer, but rather to suggest that denunciation, righteous indignation, and revolutionary appeals are vastly more prevalent in their works than in those of Douglass, Baldwin, and Ellison.

Nevertheless, when all has been said, we must recognize that both Frederick Douglass and David Walker produced works which expressed the spirit of their age but which transcend the limitations and hazards of time—works, in short, that find their counterparts in the writings of our most recent black American authors. The road for both nineteenth-century writers stretched between two alternatives that are consummately set forth in the *Narrative*:

On the one hand, there stood slavery, a stern reality, glaring frightfully upon us—its robes already crimsoned with the blood of millions, and even now feasting greedily upon our own flesh. On the other hand, away back in the dim distance, under the flickering light of the north star, behind some craggy hill or snow-covered mountain stood a doubtful freedom—half frozen—beckoning us to come and share her hospitality. [P. 92]

Both writers labored along freedom's road, under the dim light of the north star, and though they chose different modes of travel, both achieved their goals, contributing to humanity on the way.

V Men and Institutions
Booker T. Washington's Up from Slavery

This I say, not to justify slavery—on the other hand I condemn it as an institution, as we all know that in America it was established for selfish and financial reasons, and not from a missionary motive—but to call attention to a fact, and to show how Providence so often uses men and institutions to accomplish a purpose.[1]

EDUCATION—the process of developing knowledge, mind, skill, and character—has played a vital role in the black American experience. From Jamestown to the present day, black preachers, prophets, and protesters have championed the value of education in the black man's struggle for freedom and equality. Indeed, the leaders of the first black institution in America achieved their positions through education: the early church leaders were men who could lead their flocks because they possessed the ability to read and interpret the word of God as it was revealed in the Bible; moreover, they were men who had the gift of words, who could transport an audience to the heavenly kingdom all drenched in light or to the farthest depths of a terrifying hell. But the emphasis on education was not confined to men of religion; some of the most notable pioneers in protest among black Americans stressed the value of education in the salvation of the race.

David Walker, in one of the most revolutionary books ever produced by a black American, speaks thus of education:

I pray that the Lord may undeceive my ignorant brethren, and permit them to throw away pretensions, and seek after the substance of learning. I would crawl on my hands and knees through mud and mire, to the feet of a learned man, where I would sit and humbly supplicate him to instil into me, that which neither devils

[1] Booker T. Washington, *Up From Slavery*, in *Three Negro Classics*, ed. John Hope Franklin (New York, 1969), p. 37. All citations in my text are to this edition.

nor tyrants could remove, only with my life—for coloured people to acquire learning in this country makes tyrants quake and tremble on their sandy foundation.[2]

Walker felt that knowledge would show enslaved blacks exactly where they stood in relationship to their masters, and that they would consequently rise up to cut the throats of unrepentant masters. To be educated, according to his idea, was to refuse to be a slave. And Frederick Douglass takes the same point of view in his *Narrative*. After relating how one of his masters upbraided his wife for teaching him to read, Douglass says:

From that moment, I understood the pathway from slavery to freedom. It was just what I wanted, and I got it at a time when I least expected it. Whilst I was saddened by the thought of losing the aid of my kind mistress, I was gladdened by the invaluable accident, I had gained from my master. Though conscious of the difficulty of learning without a teacher, I set out with high hope, and a fixed purpose, at whatever cost of trouble, to learn how to read.[3]

Douglass devotes an entire chapter to his struggle for literacy, and, confirming Walker's theory, with increased knowledge came an increased desire for freedom.

At least two of the notable predecessors of Booker T. Washington, therefore, had observed and written about the value of education in the black man's rise from slavery. W. E. B. Du Bois had yet to speak of the contribution of those "Yankee" school "Ma'ams" who taught the freedmen during Reconstruction. In *The Souls of Black Folk*, he characterizes these early instructors of the black American race as follows:

Rich and poor they were, serious and curious. Bereaved now of a father, now of a brother, now of more than these, they came seeking a life work in planting New England schoolhouses among the white and black of the South. They did their work well. In that first year [1865] they taught one hundred thousand souls, and more.[4]

During Reconstruction, Du Bois tells us, the ideal of "book-learning" seemed to provide the "mountain path to Canaan" for black America.

[2] David Walker, *Appeal*, ed. Charles M. Wiltse (New York, 1969), pp. 31–32.

[3] Frederick Douglass, *Narrative of the Life of Frederick Douglass* (New York, 1968), p. 49.

[4] W. E. B. Du Bois, *The Souls of Black Folk*, in Franklin, *Three Negro Classics*, p. 229.

Education as a road to freedom, therefore, was an established tradition among black Americans when Booker T. Washington emerged as a leader in the late nineteenth and early twentieth centuries. In the age of Washington, however, black education had to be of a special type if it was to be tolerated by white America. By the time he had begun his life's work, blacks had, in effect, been sold out by the Hayes-Tilden Compromise of 1877; the black man was left unguarded in a South enraged by the license and licentiousness of Reconstruction. Violence against the black man, denial of his political rights, treatises on the inferiority of the race, lynchings, repression, Ku Klux Klan raids—all of these dominated the milieu that gave birth to Washington. C. Vann Woodward has chronicled the plight of the black man in the late nineteenth and early twentieth centuries, and to the abuses already mentioned adds the legalization of oppression and violence, for around the turn of the century local and national legislative bodies enacted a host of codes that were inimical to the black American.[5]

Booker T. Washington was no David Walker, willing to accept only freedom or death. Washington felt that he had formed a social and educational philosophy that was compatible with the times; through his educational labors and his public pronouncements, he attempted to show that the educated black American could be a "useful" citizen, an improver of the community, a clean and well-mannered manual laborer of high moral character. Moreover, such a black man, he insisted, would not trouble himself with social equality:

The wisest among my race understand that the agitation of questions of social equality is the extremest folly, and that progress in the enjoyment of all the privileges that will come to us must be the result of severe and constant struggle rather than of artificial forcing. No race that has anything to contribute to the markets of the world is long in any degree ostracized. It is important and right that all privileges of the law be ours, but it is vastly more important that we be prepared for the exercises of these privileges. The opportunity to earn a dollar in a factory just now is worth infinitely more than the opportunity to spend a dollar in an opera-house. [P. 149]

[5] C. Vann Woodward, *The Strange Career of Jim Crow* (New York, 1968), pp. 67–109.

The president, southern governors, and a host of politicians were grateful, enthusiastic, overwhelmed; while America went its imperialistic way in the Philippines, and while William Sumner and other race theorizers poured forth their doctrines, there was a black leader at home to keep the masses at peace. It must truly have seemed that God was in an American heaven and all was right with the Yankee world.

Even today, both revolutionaries and scholars who should know better take Washington's hand-and-finger metaphor ("In all things that are purely social we can be as separate as the fingers, yet one as the hand in all things essential to mutual progress.") as the whole of his teaching, and write off one of the most famous black Americans as a traitor on the basis of his 1895 address to the Atlanta Cotton States and International Exposition, which catapulted him to a position of national leadership. When we turn to *Up from Slavery*, however, we are forced to take another view, for Washington's autobiography is far more than an ameliorative treatise on race relations. The book is first of all a representative work in a major genre in the black literary tradition. Originally published in 1900 as *The Story of My Life and Work*, *Up from Slavery* (1901) was one of the last slave narratives published in America.

The first chapter rings a familiar note—it seems almost an imitation of Douglass's *Narrative*. The straightforwardness of the opening is the same ("I was born a slave on a plantation in Franklin County, Virginia"), the setting is again agrarian, and we see the familiar ironic equation of the status of slaves with that of the farm animals: "My mother, I suppose, attracted the attention of a purchaser who was afterward my owner and hers. Her addition to the slave family attracted about as much attention as the purchase of a new horse or cow" (p. 29). Finally, Washington assumes the "tragic mulatto" posture at the outset: "Of my father I know even less than of my mother. I do not even know his name. I have heard reports to the effect that he was a white man who lived on one of the near-by plantations" (pp. 29–30).

The similarities between Douglass and Washington are not surprising when we consider that Washington wrote one of the earliest biographies of Douglass and was familiar with his writing; nevertheless, we have similarity with a difference. Washington's view of slavery is quite unlike that of Douglass. The perspective in the first chapter of *Up from Slavery* is almost antebellum, considering the narrator's forgiving nature, his view of the positive good derived from slavery, and his discussion of the sadness felt by both master and slave when freedom arrived and parted their ways. Of his white father Washington says: "But I do not find especial fault with him. He was simply another unfortunate victim of the institution which the Nation had engrafted upon it at the time" (p. 30). On the positive good achieved by slavery, he observes that:

when we rid ourselves of prejudice, or racial feeling, and look facts in the face, we must acknowledge that, notwithstanding the cruelty and moral wrong of slavery, the ten million Negroes inhabiting this country, who themselves or whose ancestors went through the school of American slavery, are in a stronger and more hopeful condition, materially, intellectually, morally, and religiously, than is true of an equal number of black people in any other portion of the globe. [P. 37]

Heightening his antebellum tone, Washington speaks of the slave's fidelity, his willingness to lay down his life for his master, his sadness (his tears mingled with those of the master) when freedom came, and his desire, in some cases, to stay on the plantation after emancipation.

This is not to say, however, that Washington totally ignores the oppression and violence of slavery; he too talks of men reduced to brutes and treated as such, but in a tone which is, at best, compromising. More important though, is the institutional frame of mind that manifests itself throughout *Up from Slavery*. Slavery itself, as we have seen above, is designated as an "institution" and a "school," and at other points a "system" or a "net." Washington's book, therefore, like all slave narratives, begins with the "peculiar institution" of slavery, to which Washington juxtaposes another institution, the schoolhouse: "The picture of several dozen boys and girls in a schoolroom engaged in study made a deep impression upon me, and I had the feeling that to get into a schoolhouse and study in this way would be about the same as getting into paradise" (p. 32). And considering the picture of slavery that Washington presents, it is easy to see why he considered the educational institution Edenic.

Slavery was not nearly as functional as it might have been; in fact, it was out of keeping with the values of the age:

The slave system on our place, in a large measure, took the spirit of self-reliance and self-help out of the white people. . . . The slaves, of course, had little personal interest in the life of the plantation, and their ignorance prevented them from learning how to do things in the most improved and thorough manner. [P. 38]

According to Washington, the institution was a failure; unhinged gates, broken window panes, unkempt gardens, lack of refinement in diet, and general waste were the evidence of its inefficiency. The basis of Washington's condemnation is the inability of slavery to produce useful men, efficient operations, or social refinement. Ignorance, the absence of self-help, and the low value placed on self-reliance nurtured an unproductive institution. Surely the writer had imbibed his Benjamin Franklin, Ralph Waldo Emerson and Samuel Smiles, either by reading, or simply by breathing in the spirit of his age.[6]

The dichotomy between the "peculiar" institution and the educational institution continues into the second chapter of *Up from Slavery*—"Boyhood Days." While we see that the work situation could encompass educational opportunities (Washington, like Douglass, learned his letters while doing manual labor), we also see the narrator assuming the role of trickster in order to escape work and get to school on time. Moreover, Washington philosophizes on education in this chapter and tells us of his own struggle for literacy. The motivation behind his struggle is obvious; education produces merit, and "Every persecuted individual and race should get much consolation out of the great human law, which is universal and eternal, that merit, no matter under what skin found, is in the long run recognized and rewarded" (p. 50). Washington's subscription to this maxim (which seems to contain but little truth) is understandable in the light of his age: when proscription is so severe that a group's chances of upward mobility seem almost nil and when its merit is studiously ignored, one alternative to despair or revolt is to predict that "in the long run" things will be better. Washington's movement, therefore, is toward "merit" and its corresponding recognition

[6] Samuel Smiles was the author of *Self-Help* (1859). The book was a favorite in England during the entire Victorian age, and the virtues that it sets forth in many instances are the ones lauded by Washington.

and reward. At one pole of his thought stands slavery, the op-
probrious institution, and at the other stands Harvard, one of
America's oldest and most renowned universities, from which he
received an honorary degree in 1896. Institutions thus mark the
depth and height of his perspective.

In the intermediate sections of *Up from Slavery* it is still the
institution that delineates stages of development. In chapters
two and three, for example, the salt and coal mining industries
are accorded terse descriptions and negative comments. Mrs.
Ruffner's home, however, where Washington worked as a "servant," receives a positive evaluation, because here he learned
habits of cleanliness and was allowed to continue his education
while working. The major feature of the Ruffner home, in fact,
was its role as an educational institution: "the lessons that I
learned in the home of Mrs. Ruffner were as valuable to me as
any education I have ever gotten anywhere since" (p. 52). The
truth of this statement is driven home when the narrator tells
us of his cleaning the recitation room at Hampton: "It occurred
to me at once that here was my chance. Never did I receive an
order with more delight. I knew that I could sweep, for Mrs.
Ruffner had thoroughly taught me how to do that when I lived
with her" (p. 56). The significance of his accomplishment is
expressed in institutional terms: "The sweeping of that room
was my college examination, and never did any youth pass an
examination for entrance into Harvard or Yale that gave him
more genuine satisfaction" (p. 57).

From the time of his entry into college until he goes off to
found a school of his own, one institution dominates the narrative. Hampton Institute and its educational concerns are always
in the forefront in chapters three through six, and we are told
what Washington learned about helping others, recognizing the
dignity of labor, and aiding in the preparation of students (both
black and red) for study at Hampton. It is in chapter seven
"Early Days at Tuskegee," however, that we witness the start of
an interesting coalescence—the merger of a man and an institution. Washington and Tuskegee become almost inseparable for
the remainder of *Up from Slavery*.

The growth of Tuskegee parallels the progress of its founder
Still a young and inexperienced man when he went to Alabama
Washington slowly achieved recognition as his institution grew

in size and merit. We have almost a new beginning of the narrative at chapter seven, "Teaching School in a Stable and a Hen-house," since Tuskegee starts as a relatively loose-knit organization in agrarian quarters and a rural setting. As the work proceeds, however, it moves (with the school) toward greater urbanity and sophistication: the initial plantation setting becomes a "Southern Campus"; the original enrollment of thirty rural pupils becomes a body of students from twenty-seven states and territories of America and several foreign countries; the initial limited curriculum broadens to include thirty industrial departments; and the stable and henhouse become sixty-six buildings, "counting large and small." In a sense, Tuskegee almost seems to assume a life of its own; it is fed money, which is collected by Washington and his wives, and it grows into something beautiful and healthy. In fact, Washington says of Tuskegee:

One of the most encouraging signs in connection with the Tuskegee school is found in the fact that the organization is so thorough that the daily work of the school is not dependent upon the presence of any one individual. The whole executive force, including instructors and clerks, now numbers eighty-six. This force is so organized and subdivided that the machinery of the school goes on day by day like clockwork. [P. 170]

While the school is growing, its founder is given recognition and reward, and he likewise grows in stature. The man and the institution complemented each other, but it was only through a multitude of men that Washington and Tuskegee were able to survive.

In one respect, *Up from Slavery* resembles the *Autobiography* of John Stuart Mill. Mill said at the outset of his work that he not only wished to record the important events of his life, but also to acknowledge the debts he owed to the great men of his age. Washington's autobiography is filled with acknowledgements to such men: General Samuel Armstrong, A. H. Porter, President McKinley, Andrew Carnegie, President Cleveland, and Charles Eliot are only a few. If at times these names read like a patron's list for a cultural event, they do indicate the degree of recognition the author received during his life, and they represent the sources of the nourishment of Tuskegee Institute as well as the great men of Washington's acquaintance.

As the institute grew, the behavioral patterns that it encompassed were perpetuated, expounded, and affirmed by the founder before large audiences. The result, of course, is that Tuskegee came, as all institutions must, to stand for a particular behavioral pattern that was of value to the community as a whole. Those connected with, enrolled in, or responsible for the institution were considered affirmers of this pattern, and when we see some of the greatest names of Washington's time associated with Tuskegee, we can logically deduce that the school expressed, to a great extent, the values of its age. The founder condemned slavery because it stifled self-help, self-reliance, cleanliness, and efficiency—the prime values of industrial England and America. Moreover, slavery indulged ignorance and sexual license, two traits totally out of keeping with the heavily evangelical American ethic. In condemning slavery on the grounds of its un-Yankee qualities, Washington was in harmony with the traditional outlook of his country. Furthermore, in emphasizing the value of work, self-help, cleanliness, and education, he was doing no more than following the course of his age. Cleanliness has been considered an outstanding American virtue from Benjamin Franklin ("Tolerate no uncleanness in body, clothes, or habitation") to the muckrakers of the early twentieth century, and Emerson and Thoreau had written of the virtues of labor and self-help early in the nineteenth century. Placing higher education on a solid, utilitarian footing—particularly an agricultural and industrial footing (as manifest, for example, in the Morrill Act of 1862 which provided for land grant universities and vocational education)—was the goal of more notable men than we have space to mention.

In light of his traditional American point of view, it is not difficult to see why, writing in the early twentieth century, Washington chose the progression from institution to institution as a means of developing his autobiography. America itself was making exemplary institutional leaps throughout the nineteenth century, and the educational institution was particularly important. The school constitutes not only a "behavioral pattern" itself, but also an organization inculcating behavioral patterns. And Washington was able to found an institution that instilled an "American way of life" into black Americans.

Washington received perhaps his most fitting reward when

his labors were recognized by one of the oldest institutions in America. The narrator seems aware of the appropriateness and momentousness of his honorary degree from Harvard, for he even arranges his autobiography so that the 1896 Harvard commencement is described, climactically, in the last chapter, while the 1899 trip to Europe is presented in the chapter before. The founder of an educational institution that perpetuated the "American way" standing before the representatives of the oldest and one of the most renowned universities in the country to receive meet homage—this is indeed a celestial position when it is juxtaposed against that peculiar institution with which *Up from Slavery* begins. And the upward path is paved by educational institutions and the men who breathed life (money and labor) into them.

Washington thus shared the American frame of mind in regard to institution-building, and as a champion of American virtues he received fitting reward for his labors. Yet it is not difficult to discover the sources of the vociferous condemnations of the Tuskegeean. The most significant charge concerns Washington's narrowness of scope; life is reduced, particularly in the later chapters of *Up from Slavery*, to a chronicling of grants, a recording of newspaper comments on the founder's speeches and awards, and a listing of famous men met and impressed. Moreover, there is a narrowness in the very behavioral pattern that Washington endorsed, a contraction of perspective indigenous to Tuskegee Institute and its founder, a narrowness revealed in the four characteristics that mark the ideal Tuskegee graduate, the ideal Washingtonian man—skill, high moral character, a sense of expediency, and a belief in the dignity of labor (p. 200). In *Up from Slavery* there is no orientation toward the future; no cherishing of the aesthetic, the abstract, or the spiritual; there is little belief in the value of institutions beyond educational (and philanthropic) ones. More significantly, there is no social idealism looking toward a day of complete liberation, when all men shall possess their freedom as equals. In *Up from Slavery* "spirit" is translated into dollar signs, idealism into manual labor, and the desire for "freedom now" into useful work.

One hates to think what D. H. Lawrence would have made of Booker T. Washington had he turned an eye upon him in *Studies in Classic American Literature*. Washington appears

even more culpable than the Benjamin Franklin who emerges
from Lawrence's essays, for he had not only a Puritan ethical
monomania, but also a condemnatory zeal. He championed all
the American values, but also condemned those institutions that
attempted to deal with aspects of the human condition that
Tuskegee did not encompass or encourage. The church, labor
unions, political structures, idealistic educational enterprises,
and creative writing are all belittled directly or by implication
in Washington's autobiography. Commenting on one industrial
conflict, for example, the author says:

In either case, my observation convinced me that the miners were
worse off at the end of a strike. Before the days of strikes in that section of the country, I knew miners who had considerable money in
the bank, but as soon as the professional labour agitators got control,
the savings of even the more thrifty ones began disappearing. [P. 64]

In a final analysis, however, we cannot write off as a myopic
organization man the former slave who served as America's
"black leader" for twenty years, built a thriving educational institution in the heart of a racist South, and aided thousands in
the struggle for dignity. Washington's achievements would be
considered great in any age or in any country, and in late nineteenth-century America they were just short of miraculous.
Moreover, social scientists and historians such as Gunnar Myrdal,
August Meier, and Louis Harlan have demonstrated that Washington was more complex than would appear from "the ingra-
tiating mask" he presented to the world.[7] Myrdal observes that
"it is wrong to characterize Washington as an all-out accommo-
dating leader. He never relinquished the right to full equality
in all respects as the ultimate goal."[8] And Meier notes that "although overtly Washington minimized the importance of the
franchise and civil rights, covertly he was deeply involved in
political affairs and in efforts to prevent disfranchisement and

[7] Gunnar Myrdal, *An American Dilemma: The Negro Problem and Modern
Democracy* (New York, 1969), pp. 39–44; August Meier, *Negro Thought in
America, 1880–1915: Racial Ideologies in the Age of Booker T. Washington* (Ann
Arbor, Mich., 1968), pp. 110–17; Louis R. Harlan, "Booker T. Washington and the
White Man's Burden," *Booker T. Washington*, ed. Emma Lou Thornbrough
(Englewood Cliffs, N.J., 1969), pp. 167–73. Harlan is currently preparing a de-
finitive biography of Washington, and his *The Papers of Booker T. Washington*
(in fifteen volumes) will soon be released by the University of Illinois Press.
[8] Myrdal, p. 739.

other forms of discrimination."[9] Finally, Harlan points out that "those who have thought of Booker T. Washington as a provincial southern American Negro, intellectually as well as geographically isolated from the rest of the world, will be surprised to find that he was substantially involved in African affairs."[10] The Booker T. Washington Papers in the Library of Congress have come under increasing scrutiny, and apparently Washington's private writings portray a man at variance with the public spokesman. Meier, for example, points out that he secretly agitated against lynching and goes on to prove that he was a skilled politician and grantsman who obtained noteworthy appointments and donations for those black Americans whom he deemed worthy of recognition and reward.[11]

Further research is likely to modify our overall evaluation of the man, but new information cannot alter *Up from Slavery*. The social philosophy set forth in this autobiography and the manner in which it is presented indicate that the author was not as fine a champion of black American rights as he might have been. At a time when the broadest possible perspective and the greatest aid were needed in the black man's struggle for freedom and equality, Washington failed in one of the primary roles of the leader. He opened too few of the doors toward his followers' most sought-after goal; in fact, he closed the doors and barred the shutters on all that lay beyond the ultimate welfare and informing philosophy of his own autonomous, somewhat mechanized institution. By championing the value of education, however, and by producing a sort of Horatio Alger handbook of how to acquire an education and how to set up an educational institution, Washington was following in the path of men such as Walker and Douglass, and anticipating Du Bois. In any meaningful examination of black literature and culture it is impossible to ignore *Up from Slavery*, the book that presents the man Washington and the institution Tuskegee.

9 Meier, p. 110.
10 Harlan, p. 167.
11 Meier, pp. 110–15.

VI The Black Man of Culture
W. E. B. Du Bois and The Souls of Black Folk

HE bright ideals of the past,—physical freedom, political
power, the training of brains and the training of hands,—all
these in turn have waxed and waned, until even the last grows
dim and overcast. Are they all wrong,—all false? No, not that, but
each alone was oversimple and incomplete,—the dreams of a credulous race-childhood, or the fond imaginings of the other world
which does not know and does not want to know our power. To be
really true, all these ideals must be melted and welded into one.[1]

Thus spoke W. E. B. Du Bois, the herald of a new age in
the history of the black American, and the statement tells a
good deal about Du Bois's point of view. Du Bois was conscious of the ideals of the past in the black American experience, and he recognized their value. He felt that a new stage in
the growth of the black man in America had been reached, and
he believed there had to be a synthesis of the ideals of the past, a
synthesis that would lead to the manhood of the black American
race. The realization of the "pastness of the past" and the sense
of a new age that inform *The Souls of Black Folk* are not surprising when one considers that Du Bois was a man of the twentieth-century—he died in the last decade. The more interesting
part of the statement is the portion that deals with synthesis, the
melting and welding of a wide range of ideas into a broader and
more effective whole; for it is his stand as a synthesizer that
marks Du Bois as a man of culture.

The word *culture*, as Raymond Williams[2] has insisted, is a
protean entity, but Du Bois seems to belong to a tradition of the
cultured man that was perhaps best characterized by Matthew
Arnold. Both Arnold and Du Bois, along with men like Walter
Pater and Oscar Wilde, seem to express a similar point of view

1 W. E. B. Du Bois, *The Souls of Black Folk*, in *Three Negro Classics*, ed. John
Hope Franklin (New York, 1969), pp. 219–20. All citations in my text are to this
edition.

2 Raymond Williams, *Culture and Society, 1780–1950* (New York, 1958).

when they speak of culture and the cultural man. For Du Bois and Arnold, culture consisted of the study of harmonious perfection and the acquisition and diffusion of "the best that has been thought and known in the world . . . [in order] to make all men live in an atmosphere of sweetness and light."[3]

It encompassed a knowledge of the classics, a grounding in broad human sympathies, and a struggle for self-realization through the arts of the Western world. The cultured man is elevated above the scenes of clerical and secular life; he is at some remove from the people, a man of astute sensibility who can wisely and justly criticize the state of society. In short, he was for Du Bois a "Negro intellectual," and to a certain extent *The Souls of Black Folk* is a prototype for Harold Cruse's recent work.

In defining the Negro intellectual, Du Bois drew from a tradition that played a large part in European and American civilization during the last decades of the nineteenth century; not only was Arnold's idea of culture involved, but also the aestheticism of men like Pater, Wilde, and a host of others in Britain, France, and America. Although the *fin de siècle* saw some outrageous poets and a few delicate poseurs, there were also a number of writers who felt that "art for art's sake" meant art for culture's sake. Many writers believed that the products of the intellect and the imagination, if properly handled, could lead to self-realization; from the individual who possessed this virtue it was but a short step to a better society. These writers were in the front ranks of those who looked to "culture" as a court of appeal above the sometimes grim realities of an industrial age; for them the word culture denoted an ethereal substance or process that had little to do with "a whole way of life" engaged in by a specific, homogeneous group of people. Oscar Wilde, Pater's chief disciple, expressed all of these points in his collection *Intentions*.

Du Bois frequently prefaces or intersperses his essays with quotations from the aesthetic school, and the tone of many of his passages is that of decadence—of the passing of the old order, with a hint of ominous events to come. But the *raison d'être* for the black man of culture is what connects Du Bois's point of view with a well-defined tradition. The cultured man will insure

3 Matthew Arnold, *Culture and Anarchy*, ed. J. Dover Wilson (Cambridge, 1963), pp. 48, 70.

the growth and harmonious progress of America. At several points in *The Souls of Black Folk*, Du Bois emerges as a fervent nationalist championing the ideal of human brotherhood—a sort of classical harmony of souls. In his first essay, for example, he advocates "the ideal of fostering and developing the traits and talents of the Negro, not in opposition to or contempt for other races, but rather in large conformity to the greater ideals of the American Republic, in order that some day on American soil two world-races may give each to each those characteristics both so sadly lack" (p. 220). The black man of culture is in a position to contribute to the welfare of society as a whole.

Du Bois's delineation of the cultured man as an asset to the American Republic is best seen in two essays—"Of the Training of Black Men" and "Of the Sons of Master and Man." In the first essay, he traces the development of black education and concludes that the most influential early educators saw that it was necessary to have a group of college-bred black men before the education of the entire race could be achieved, for such men ran the common, normal, and industrial schools. The growth of black education had to commence at the college level, at such schools as Fisk, Howard, Atlanta, and Shaw. Du Bois goes on to state that whites doubted the wisdom of giving blacks a college education since they felt it would unfit blacks for "useful" work, but he demonstrates that the majority of black men who received B.A. degrees were productive citizens—teachers, physicians, civil servants, and artisans. Du Bois then points out the sterling merits of educated black men:

Comparing them as a class with my fellow students in New England and in Europe, I cannot hesitate in saying that nowhere have I met men and women with a broader spirit of helpfulness, with deeper devotion to their life-work, or with more consecrated determination to succeed in the face of bitter difficulties than among Negro college-bred men. [P. 280]

The blacks of whom he speaks, moreover, are cultured men, men of "larger vision and deeper sensibility" (p. 280). And they offer one solution to the American racial problem, for Du Bois felt that ". . . the present social separation and acute race-sensitiveness must eventually yield to the influences of culture [i.e., the arts and artifacts of the West and the way of life they project], as the South grows more civilized. . . ." (p. 281). More significant to Du Bois, however, is the fact that black men of culture generally make "conservative, careful leaders"; they are men who have withstood the temptation to lead the mob and have worked steadily and faithfully in the South. The implications of this statement are obvious, and they bring out a remarkable similarity between Du Bois's point of view and the outlook of Booker T. Washington.

Du Bois sets the black man of culture up as a stop gap between the masses and the progress of society; such a man will stress nonviolent political activities, the rectification of economic ills, and educational ideals that will keep the millions from brooding over the wrongs of the past and the difficulties of the present.[4] If the "Talented Tenth" of the race is not recognized and allowed to lead, Du Bois feels the results are foreordained:

. . . as the black third of the land grows in thrift and skill, unless skillfully guided in its larger philosophy, it must more and more brood over the red past and the creeping, crooked present, until it grasps a gospel of revolt and revenge and throws its new-found energies athwart the current of advance. [P. 282]

This gospel is a long way from the militant revolutionary syndrome of our own time. Of course, "A Litany at Atlanta," the poem that Du Bois wrote in response to the Atlanta race riot of 1906, could be offered as a counter to this statement, for a life that spans nearly a century must possess its restless turnings and

---

4 Saunders Redding states, in *"The Souls of Black Folk*: Du Bois' Masterpiece Lives On," *Black Titan: W. E. B. Du Bois*, ed. John Henrik Clarke (Boston, 1970), pp. 47–51, that *The Souls of Black Folk* "not only represented a profound change in its scholar-author's view of what was then called the 'Negro Problem'; but heralded a new approach to social reform on the part of the American Negro people—an approach of patriotic, nonviolent activism which achieved its first success a decade ago." According to Redding, Du Bois's collection was as influential in determining the strategies of liberation of the last two decades as Gandhi's resistance in India, the 1954 Supreme Court decision, and the work of Martin Luther King. While this is an overstatement, it must be acknowledged that Du Bois's point of view has been adopted (to a greater or lesser extent) by a number of prominent black leaders since the second decade of this century. As one of the founders and long-term officers of the National Association for the Advancement of Colored People and as editor of its journal, *The Crisis*, Du Bois provided a living example of the type of guidance and the patterns of action that he called for in *The Souls of Black Folk*. Such men as James Weldon Johnson, Walter White, Roy Wilkins, the late Whitney Young, and James Farmer have shared Du Bois's educational ideals and have attempted to position themselves as buffers between the latent rage of the black masses and the progress of American society.

abrupt shifts. And Du Bois's career was no exception. He moved from essential agreement with Booker T. Washington to almost total disagreement, from the Niagara Movement and the National Association for the Advancement of Colored People to socialism, from a moderate socialism to membership in the Communist party, and from the United States to Africa where he died as a Ghanaian citizen. One of the most important aspects of *The Souls of Black Folk*, however, is its delineation of the black man of culture as a mediator between opposing sides of the American veil. Some of Du Bois's highly-rhetorical conclusions would make today's revolutionaries cringe: "I sit with Shakespeare and he winces not. Across the color line I move arm in arm with Balzac and Dumas, where smiling men and welcoming women glide in gilded halls. . . . So, wed with truth, I dwell above the Veil" (p. 284).

The second essay, "Of the Sons of Masters and Man," offers a further instance of Du Bois's elevated stance. After dealing in sociological terms with the question of personal contact between blacks and whites in the South, Du Bois concludes that the "best" of the two races seldom come together in economic, educational, political, or religious activities; in fact, the "best" men of each group normally encounter only the worst of the other. This situation, according to Du Bois, is inimical to progress; as long as both groups continue to see only each other's worst aspects, the old myths of black inferiority and white insipidity and indifference will remain. In effect, Du Bois champions a sort of "house servant" perspective, for he feels that during slavery the best of the whites and the best of the blacks did get together in the "big house"; after slavery, moreover, the black domestics (who were the best blacks of their time according to Du Bois) still came into contact with the "best" white families of the South. The tragedy of twentieth century society, Du Bois feels, is that the "color-line" has been drawn so strictly that it excludes from polite society not only the black lower class, but also the truly deserving black men of culture.

Such a situation was deplorable partly because it meant that the most competent leaders of the black masses were not fulfilling their proper roles. Like the liberals of the nineteenth century, Du Bois hesitated to ask for unconditional equality and unrestricted freedom; his demand was primarily that a sort of Washingtonian "merit" be recognized and rewarded. If classification was necessary to differentiate the high from the low, the leaders from the laborers, Du Bois was all for classification: "Draw lines of crime, of incompetency, of vice, as tightly and uncompromisingly as you will, for these things must be proscribed; but a color-line not only does not accomplish the purpose, but thwarts it" (p. 336). And while arguing for finer sympathies and broader understanding, Du Bois even enters a Washingtonian apology for the best traditions of the South:

I freely acknowledge that it is possible, and sometimes best, that a partially developed people should be ruled by the best of their stronger and better neighbors for their own good, until such time as they can start and fight the world's battles alone . . . and I am quite willing to admit that if the representatives of the best white Southern public opinion were the ruling and guiding power in the South to-day the conditions indicated [economic and spiritual guidance for the black masses] would be fairly well fulfilled. [P. 329]

Du Bois felt, however, that the educated black men of his day were in a position to take over the job of guiding and leading the masses; they had only to be recognized by the "best white Southern public opinion" and allowed to assume the job. To this end public opinion had to be informed through social intercourse with the black man of culture (over a "social cigar and a cup of tea"). The result of the cultural man's leadership, of course, would be the advancement of the nation and the spiritual improvement of the masses, for Du Bois argues that once it is granted that individual black men have the ability to "assimilate the culture and common sense of modern civilization, and to pass it on, to some extent at least, to their fellows," certain assumptions can be made:

If this is true, then here is the path out of the economic situation, and here is the imperative demand for trained Negro leaders of character and intelligence—men of skill, men of light and leading, college-bred men, black captains of industry, and missionaries of culture; men who thoroughly comprehend and know modern civilization, and can take hold of Negro communities and raise and train them by force of precept and example, deep sympathy, and the inspiration of common blood and ideals. [P. 326]

At least two other essays in *The Souls of Black Folk* define the black man of culture and his role in modern society—"Of the

Wings of Atalanta" and "Of the Quest of the Golden Fleece."
In both pieces, Du Bois presents culture and the cultured man
as foils to materialism, as did Arnold in, *Culture and Anarchy*.
Men trained in the things of the intellect and imagination can
aid in the salvation of a land of "dust and dollars" by guiding
the beautifully ideal Atalanta away from the fatal golden apples.
In the second essay, Du Bois again poses the tragic results of
the South's quest for cotton, the golden fleece, and the beneficial
counterinfluences of culture.

The definition of the cultural man's role seems not only justifiable, but also ideal. A great many people in Du Bois's age
believed that certain artistic and intellectual pursuits could lead
to the improvement of society through individual self-realization.
Yet some qualifications are in order. While elevating the black
intellectual, Du Bois perhaps depressed the masses too far.
Throughout *The Souls of Black Folk*, one finds invidious distinctions between the man of culture and all black people who
inhabit the realms "beneath" him. One finds the author speaking
of the "black lowly," "Sambo," the "black peasantry," and the
"black crowd gaudy and dirty." These terms might have acted
only as heuristic epithets reinforcing Du Bois's argument, but
he made it indubitably clear that he believed the man of culture
was qualitatively better than the next man. In one essay, for
example, he makes a distinction between "honest toil" and "dignified manhood," a distinction that seems to place the worker in
a subhuman category. And this dichotomy is further emphasized
when the author speaks of a "reverent comradeship between the
black lowly and the black *men* emancipated by training and
culture" [my italics]. Moreover, in "Of the Coming of John,"
one is led to feel sympathy only for John, the tragic black man
of culture who is not accepted by whites and who is too elevated
to communicate with his own people—"the ignorant and turbu-
lent" black proletariat.

Du Bois's cultured contempt for Washington, moreover, lends
credence to the charge that he was overzealous in championing
the black intellectual. In "Of Mr. Booker T. Washington and
Others," he assumes an almost perfectly Arnoldian approach to
criticism; denying any envy of Washington, he asserts that he
must denounce the Tuskegeean for the good of the country. In
evaluating some of the ways in which black Americans have

dealt with the experience of slavery and its aftermath, Du Bois writes off two categories—the submissive and the militantly revolutionary—as ineffectual, then goes on to link Nat Turner, Denmark Vesey, and Gabriel Prosser with the colonizationists (who wished to send blacks "home" to Africa), while placing Washington, rather abruptly, in the submissive category. Washington emerges as a man who has sold out the rights of his people, who has forfeited the black man's demands for political power, civil rights, and higher education. Moreover, he is presented as a leader whose career was paralleled by a retrogression of his followers and whose leadership was "imposed" from the outside on an unwilling people. Finally, Washington's entire career comes to be viewed as a paradox, and the man himself as a submissive compromiser, a somewhat naive, proletarian Uncle Tom. And Du Bois's picture of Washington has had a succession of admirers.

The irony of this portrait, however, is that many of the charges that Du Bois levels against Washington have a double edge: they turn and cut the author himself. While insisting that Washington's leadership was imposed from the outside, Du Bois seems surprisingly unaware that he himself is a Harvard man addressing the nation in sophisticated prose. Speaking of the lack of "self-assertion" and "self-respect" in Washington's philosophy, Du Bois seems willfully to ignore the fact that one of Washington's key concepts was that of "self-help," an important element in the same liberal tradition that informs much of *The Souls of Black Folk*. While condemning Washington's concessions to white America, Du Bois speaks in rhapsodic tones of the American "Fatherland." While belittling Washington's failure to demand all the rights that belong to the black American, Du Bois himself condones a conditional sufferage and states that black universities should be dwellings for "the best of the Negro youth."

This, of course, is neither to say that Du Bois's charges lack validity, nor that the picture he presents is totally inaccurate. The multiple ironies of Du Bois's portrait simply illustrate that what he says of Washington's philosophy is equally true of his own: it contains many "half truths." Washington is not given credit for the great work he accomplished in the South, and Tuskegee is not seen as a fine and productive institution. The fact that Washington's achievements are understated in Du Bois's account simply marks the author once again as a man who made somewhat invidious distinctions, a man who (despite his breadth of vision) was sometimes unable to see those below his cultural level in a fair light. Washington, after all, was not a "college-bred" man in Du Bois's estimation. A proletarian, capitalistic, submissive Washington, therefore, is set against a self-assertive, broad-minded, thoughtful, patriotic, sympathetic black intellectual.

Dudley Randall's humorous poem, "Booker T. and W. E. B.," captures what seems to be a prevailing view of Washington and Du Bois:

> "It seems to me," said Booker T.,
> "It shows a mighty lot of cheek
> To study chemistry and Greek
> When Mister Charlie needs a hand
> To hoe the cotton on his land,
> And when Miss Ann looks for a cook,
> Why stick your nose inside a book?"
>
> "I don't agree," said W. E. B.
> "If I should have the drive to seek
> Knowledge of chemistry or Greek,
> I'll do it. Charles and Miss can look
> Another place for hand or cook.
> Some men rejoice in skill of hand,
> And some in cultivating land,
> But there are others who maintain
> The right to cultivate the brain."
>
> "It seems to me," said Booker T.,
> "That all you folks have missed the boat
> Who shout about the right to vote,
> And spend vain days and sleepless nights
> In uproar over civil rights.
> Just keep your mouths shut, do not grouse,
> But work, and save, and buy a house."
>
> "I don't agree," said W. E. B.,
> "For what can property avail
> If dignity and justice fail?
> Unless you help to make the laws,
> They'll steal your house with trumped-up clause.
> A rope's as tight, a fire as hot,

No matter how much cash you've got.
Speak soft, and try your little plan,
But as for me, I'll be a man."

"It seems to me," said Booker T.——

"I don't agree,"
Said W. E. B.[5]

The point of view that Du Bois expressed in *The Souls of Black Folk*, however, was as far removed from that of the majority of black Americans in 1903 as was Booker T. Washington's. At the turn of the century, approximately ninety per cent of black Americans lived in poverty in the deep South, and an industrial education and self-help were just as far beyond their ken and their economic means as an education in the best that had been thought and known in the Western world or an effective non-violent campaign for civil rights. What qualified Du Bois's philosophy for praise and permanence was its attention to the true folk experience of the black American and its orientation toward the future. Washington's outlook was grounded in its age, and it tended to revise the folk experience along lines acceptable to "the best white Southern public opinion." With his broader vision and deeper sensibility, his training at Fisk, Harvard, and the University of Berlin, Du Bois was able to survey the black American experience through the lenses of sociology, philosophy, history, and creative literature. A man gifted with high intellectual abilities, Du Bois was seldom subject to the type of critical myopia that beset Washington when he was asked to conceive of patterns of action not encompassed by the ruling philosophy of Tuskegee.

At times Du Bois's stance as a man of culture caused him to treat the masses of black America unjustly, but this same point of view enabled him to grasp the essential character of the black American folk experience. While studying in Berlin under Gustav Schmoller (1892–94), Du Bois came to believe that the solution to the American racial problem was "a matter of systematic investigation," and throughout his life he was dedicated to critical objectivity—to what Matthew Arnold defined as "disinterestedness." The critic could achieve this ideal, according to

5 In *Black Voices*, ed. Abraham Chapman (New York, 1968), pp. 470–71.

Arnold, "by keeping aloof from what is called 'the practical view of things'; by resolutely following the law of [criticism's] own nature, which is to be a free play of the mind on all subjects which it touches."[6] Du Bois allowed his mind to play freely on all facets of the black experience, and the results were often praise and admiration.

In *The Souls of Black Folk* he pays tribute to the black church ("Of the Faith of Our Fathers"), to black leaders ("Of Alexander Crummell"), to the black folk who have striven to meliorate their condition (Josie in "Of the Meaning of Progress"), and to the spirit of endurance and beauty that has always characterized black folk culture ("Of Our Spiritual Strivings," "Of the Sorrow Songs"). In short, Du Bois broadened the Arnoldian definition of culture, which was narrowly white and Western, to include the best that had been thought and known in the world of the black American folk. By bringing his critical and creative abilities to bear on black America he was able to see where the true strength of that culture, of that whole way of life, lay: in its ability to create beauty from wretchedness, intellectuals from victims of slavery, and viable institutions from rigidly proscribed patterns of action. Du Bois employed the methods of careful scholarships, yet he conveyed his findings in a beautifully lyrical prose style:

Such [black] churches are really governments of men, and consequently a little investigation reveals the curious fact that, in the South, at least, practically every American Negro is a church member. Some, to be sure, are not regularly enrolled, and a few do not habitually attend services; but, practically, a proscribed people must have a social centre, and that centre for this people is the Negro church. [P. 341]

Throughout *The Souls of Black Folk* there are such passages (indeed, entire essays) that pulsate with knowledge of the folk and with the oracular Biblical tones of the prophet. The diction is literary, and the intended audience (given the condition of the majority of black Americans in 1903) was either white America or the educated elite of black America, but the sentiments expressed proceed directly out of the folk experience. Du Bois, in

---

[6] Matthew Arnold, "The Function of Criticism at the Present Time," in *Criticism: The Major Texts*, ed. Walter Jackson Bate (New York, 1952), p. 458.

fact, was only one of a number of black intellectuals who at the turn of the century began the task of transcribing the values and achievements of an oral, folk experience into the cultured and written forms known to only a few black Americans.[7]

The number of black college-bred men and women was destined to increase, however, and Du Bois and other turn-of-the-century intellectuals were destined to become their models and their leaders. By the time of the Harlem Renaissance, the ideal of the cultured man had become a norm in the black American experience, and Du Bois was a seminal influence. Ernest Kaiser states that "Du Bois' works were part of the background for the Harlem Renaissance of the 1920s and early thirties. Du Bois participated in this movement as the encouraging editor of *The Crisis* during this period, and as the author of the essay 'The Black Man Brings His Gifts,' published in Alain Locke's *The New Negro* (1925) and of the novel *Dark Princess* (1928)."[8] The literary and social life of black America during the Renaissance was influenced and guided by such men as Countee Cullen, Alain Locke, Wallace Thurman, Charles S. Johnson, Arna Bontemps, and Langston Hughes—all of whom were well educated and aware of the value of Western culture, and were not averse to criticizing blacks in works that are sometimes scathing in their satire (for example, Cullen's *One Way to Heaven* and Thurman's *The Blacker the Berry* and *Infants of the Spring*). The majority of the writers and scholars of the Harlem Renaissance, however, were as acculturated as Du Bois himself; their perspectives were broadened and enriched by a knowledge of black folk culture. The poetry of Langston Hughes, Claude McKay's *Home to Harlem*, the short stories of Rudolph Fisher, James Weldon Johnson's *God's Trombones* and many other works of the Harlem Renaissance celebrate the survival values and the lyrical beauty of the folk experience.

Finally, one has only to survey the works of Richard Wright, Ralph Ellison, and James Baldwin to see that the norm of the black man of culture established for this century by W. E. B.

7 Others were James Weldon Johnson, Charles Chesnutt, Paul Laurence Dunbar, William Monroe Trotter, Archibald Grimké, Carter G. Woodson, and J. Rosamond Johnson.
8 Ernest Kaiser, "Cultural Contributions of Dr. Du Bois," in Clarke, *Black Titan*, p. 71.

Du Bois has played a significant role in contemporary black American culture. Wright, Ellison, and Baldwin have adopted a detached [cultured] point of view; employed standard, literary prose; and chosen characteristically Western literary forms for their work. Like Du Bois, however, each writer was open to the free play of ideas, and this led to an acculturative experience. In works such as *Native Son, Invisible Man,* and *Go Tell It on the Mountain,* the arts, institutions, and leaders of black America are normally lauded for their role in insuring the survival and growth of a culture and in providing maturation and value for its artists. The invocation that concludes *The Souls of Black Folk* has been answered: "Hear my cry, O God the Reader; vouchsafe that this my book fall not still-born into the world wilderness." The book had little chance of falling still-born. The whole way of life that it ultimately celebrates has continued to grow in strength and beauty, and the author's stance as a black man of culture and a transcriber of folk values has provided a paradigm for several generations of black artists and intellectuals.

VII   From the Improbable Fields Down South

One View of Ghetto Language and Culture

> . . . *Plantations,*
> *learning America,*
> *as speech, and a common emptiness* . . .
>
> Le Roi Jones

IN ONE of the most memorable scenes in *Go Tell It on the Mountain*, John Grimes, covered with dust from a "heavy red and green and purple oriental-style carpet," gazes at pictures of his ancestors from "the improbable fields down south." A few pages later in the book, he stands on the summit of a hill in Central Park and stares with awe at the city below. The contrasting images of agrarian past and urban present are so skillfully drawn and proximate that they blend into a complex emblem which is reinforced throughout the novel.

Since the first massive migration of blacks to the North in response to America's industrial needs during World War I, a fundamental problem for the black American has been his attempt to adjust to the city's garish lights, its swift-moving and brutal crowds, and its faces that hold no love for him. In our century black Americans have poured into cities in ever-increasing numbers, and given the separatist character of American society, it is not surprising that most of this country's major cities contain clearly-defined black sections. These sections are sometimes euphemistically called *bronzeville* or *smoketown*, but their simplest designation is *black ghetto*.

The word *ghetto* normally brings visions of a besieged Warsaw or a riot-torn Newark and produces clichés, fashionable guilt, or philanthropic condolences. If we consider the scholarly works that have been written about ghetto culture during the past seventy years, we can understand this response. From W. E. B. DuBois's *The Philadelphia Negro* (1899) through Oscar Lewis's *The Children of Poverty* (1961), students of ghetto life have been presented with an image of the impoverished, present-oriented, pleasure-seeking, illiterate, ofttimes violent and socially determined outsider as the archetypal ghetto dweller. Studies by E. Franklin Frazier, Gunnar Myrdal, Horace Clayton, and Sinclair Drake emphasize the passivity and other-directedness of ghetto dwellers, and the focus on the passivity of the black male has been accompanied by a concern for the ghetto female and the matriarchal family. Both Frazier and Daniel Patrick Moynihan have painted bleak pictures of the broken ghetto family, the irresponsible ghetto male, and the somewhat Faulknerian ghetto mother who holds the tenuous threads of the family together. What this portrayal amounts to, in terms of the black American ghetto, is the application of images drawn from the fields down south to a complex urban scene which they now fail to elucidate.

In fact, the outlines of this traditional picture of passivity began to waver during the 1964 Harlem riot, and after holocausts had swept Watts, Oklahoma City, and Newark. The mass media showed stern, active, and embittered men who bore little resemblance to the passive black migrants delineated by a host of studies. In consequence of this, the focus began to shift to the active component of ghetto life, the black man of the inner city; and Lee Rainwater, succinctly describes this new perspective:

This focus perfectly mirrored, and was perhaps also stimulated by, the shift from primarily passive images of Negroes that were congenial to traditional Southern-oriented race studies to more aggressive images congenial to studies in the big Northern cities particularly as, one by one, they were struck by ghetto riots.[1]

At present, many social scientists refuse to view the black ghetto as a passive, externally-directed environment; rather, they consider it to be the home of a unique, dynamic, and open-ended culture. Most have come to the realization that lower-class black urban culture differs from both "the culture of poverty" and American immigrant cultures such as the Jewish, Chinese, and Italian. Robert Blauner, for example, points out that

When an ethnic culture is strong or when political working-class consciousness is cultivated (as [Oscar] Lewis believes has taken place

[1] Introduction to *Black Experience: Soul*, ed. Lee Rainwater (Chicago, 1970), p. 9.

among the Cuban poor), the culture of poverty with all its negative effects declines. If Lewis is correct—and he makes sense to me—the black culture and the black power movements among American Negroes may represent the strengthening of ethnic consciousness, the ethnic culture component, at the expense of lower-class culture.[2]

Blauner goes on to show how the acculturation of black American history has been infinitely more complex than the cultural process of any American immigrant group. The Chinese and the Italians, for example, have moved from extranational status to an ethnic culture and then to assimilation, and a decline in ethnicity has accompanied their assimilation. Black Americans, on the other hand, were subjected to an "almost total 'absorption' or forced acculturation without the group autonomy, social and economic equality that accompanied assimilation for other minorities."[3] This means that there has been a general reversal in the direction of the black American cultural process: black Americans have moved from forced acculturation to ethnicity, and the process has been complicated by an interplay of diverse sources.

Slavery, the southern way of life, Emancipation, and northern migration, have all complicated the black cultural process. The most overwhelming factor, of course, has been American racism, for though we can demonstrate the similarities between the black, urban ghetto and the immigrant ghetto, we are forced to admit that the former is

. . . less a voluntary community; it serves to segregate the mass of Afro-Americans from a racist society which resists the assimilation of darker peoples. This may be why Negro ghettos have been the setting for the development of distinct ethnic traits and group solidarity, whereas the immigrant ghettos were actually way-stations in the process of acculturation and assimilation.[4]

Since the institutions and the modes of adaptation of the black American ghetto are clearly not those of the mainstream culture and differ significantly from other lower-class or minority cultures, it seems that we can posit a separate and distinct black

---

2 Robert Blauner, "The Question of Black Culture," in *Black America*, ed. John F. Szwed (New York, 1970), p. 117.

3 *Ibid.*, p. 112.

4 *Ibid.*, p. 114.

American culture whose ambit is the inner city. This postulate does not deny the meaningful similarities between black American culture and other cultures, but it does alter our response to the term "black ghetto." Clichés, guilt, and condolences will no longer do; serious research has become the order of the day. Thus, the adjustment of the empirical vision to include an active component of black ghetto life has produced an entirely new area of scholarship.

When charismatic and militant black men like Stokeley Carmichael, H. Rap Brown, Malcolm X, and Huey P. Newton stepped into the forefront of the liberation struggle in the 1960s, the quiescense of what Du Bois called "eloquent omissions and silences" surrounding the black man was broken, and Mr. Tambo and Mr. Bones—those images of the black man accepted for more than a generation—took flight. It has become clear that black Americans not only possess a unique culture, but are also unique and dynamic transmitters of that culture. These holders of the black American legacy have been variously labelled "street-corner males," "block men," and "cool people," but behind this diversity is a trait they hold in common: they all fit Roger Abrahams's definition of the "man-of-words." Just as Carmichael, Brown, and Newton gained the national spotlight through their ability to hold the stage verbally in the ghettos, so the respected "street-corner male" gains local prominence by the same means. He is a figure who, according to Abrahams, plays an important role in many black communities:

This ability of a person to use active and copious verbal performance to achieve recognition within his group is observable throughout Afro-American communities in the New World. It has given rise to an observable social type which I have elsewhere called the "man-of-words." His performances are typified by his willingness to entertain and instruct anywhere and anytime, to make his own occasions.[5]

The man-of-words embodies, champions, and projects something which is highly cherished in the black American cultural tradition—an expressive life style which is currently subsumed under the heading "soul." The black man-of-words is a person who —through his inventive talk—transmits attitudes and values that

5 Roger D. Abrahams, "Rapping and Capping: Black Talk as Art," in Szwed, *Black America*, p. 134.

have assured the adaptation and survival of the race; he is the agent of a *sui generis* culture that can be fully understood only when we comprehend his language.

The language employed by street-corner male society in the black ghetto has its origins, like most institutions of black culture, in those improbable fields down south mentioned by Baldwin; and, again like most institutions in the culture, its evolution has been greatly influenced by the separatism of mainstream American culture. William Stewart sees the beginnings of present-day ghetto language in the black American slaves' acquisition of English.[6] Slaves from the same tribes in West Africa were separated when they arrived in America in order to minimize the chances of rebellion; those on the same small farm or plantation could not communicate with one another until they had developed a *lingua franca*, which in most cases was a pidginized English similar to the *patois* spoken today by blacks in the West Indies and on the Gullah Islands off the coast of South Carolina and Georgia. This language was also acquired by the American Indians, since whites tended to communicate with all nonwhites in the same tongue, and many of the features of the language have been passed on from generation to generation in the development of black American culture. Such features as the use of the objective pronoun for both the subjective and objective cases, the absence of the verb *to be*, and the use of the past tense only at the beginning of a narration can be observed in the speech of Gullah Island and Harlem children today. The influence of the first separate and distinct language acquired by slaves has been so prevalent that "research currently going on all over the country seems to make it clear that in no part of the United States do Negroes and whites speak identically; this is especially true of Negroes of a lower socioeconomic class."[7]

The differences between the language of the man-of-words in today's black ghetto and standard English go well beyond the grammatical. The radically different ethos surrounding the use of language in the black ghetto is as much responsible for its variance from standard English as the employment of black slang words and variant linguistic features by ghetto inhabitants.

6 William A. Stewart, "Understanding Black Language," in Szwed, *Black America*, pp. 121–30.
7 *Ibid.*, p. 125.

Thomas Kochman, in fact, distinguishes six different genres of
ghetto talk, only one of which—running it down—is designed to
perform the primary function of standard English, the communication of instruction and information.[8] The other genres that
Kochman lists—rapping and capping, shucking and jiving, gripping and copping a plea, signifying, and playing or sounding—
are "directive" linguistic forms, structured to persuade a listener,
to gain some material benefit, or to motivate action in a static
situation. Thus "rapping" may be designed to convince a "fox"
to join a pimp's stable, to "work the Murphy" (sell a customer
the services of a nonexistent prostitute), or to create a favorable
impression on a peer at the beginning of a relationship. Shucking and jiving may be employed to "put on Whitey" or to dupe
one's peers. Copping a plea or gripping is used to minimize the
harmful effects of a fearful situation, and signifying is employed
to motivate a contest between two people in a static situation.
"Playing" or "sounding" is designed to release hostilities by
engaging in a verbal contest where adversaries abuse each other's
families, the primary target being the mother.

An example of a pimp's rap and a "capping" incident in a
bout of the dozens helps to illustrate the nature of ghetto language. The pimp is rapping to an ex-whore:

[I said:] "Now try to control yourself baby. I'm the tall stud with
the bedroom eyes across the hall in four-twenty. I'm the guy with the
pretty towel wrapped around his sexy hips. I got the same hips on now
that you X-rayed. Remember that hunk of sugar your peepers
feasted on?"

She said: "Maybe, but you shouldn't call me. I don't want an incident. What do you want? A lady doesn't accept phone calls from
strangers."

I said: "A million dollars and a trip to the moon with a bored,
trapped, beautiful bitch, you dig? I'm no stranger. I've been popping
the elastic on your panties ever since you saw me in the hall. . . ."[9]

The "capping" incident was related by one of Abrahams's
informants:

[8] Thomas Kochman, "Rapping in the Ghetto," in Rainwater, *Black Experience:
Soul*, pp. 51–76.

[9] *Ibid.*, p. 54. The incident occurs in *Pimp: The Story of My Life*, by Iceberg
Slim [Robert Beck] (Los Angeles, 1967).

Now I wasn't there, but everyone was talking about it. They were playing the dozens; Darrel was capping on Sam consistently. Sam was letting it build up to a peak, you know, letting Darrel be the instigator. So finally Sam stopped him and asked him did his mother love him? Darrel was shocked and didn't think and just responded naturally and said "Yes," and Sam answered him as if he was just throwing it off. He said, "That's right, all bitches love their puppies."[10]

In both examples, the language is directive and persuasive; once the audience is envisioned, the successful results can be well imagined. It seems obvious that such speakers would gain a large measure of respect from their fellows. In a situation where property ownership is rare, employment scarce, excitement minimal, and literacy sparse, but where talk is abundant, it seems natural that status is conferred according to verbal ability. Moreover, when the conscious artifice that accompanies the genres Kochman sets forth is considered, Abrahams's designation of black talk as art seems justified. The ability to "dance" one's talk, to dramatize the self by the use of an intrusive first person pronoun, to employ aggressive and active verbs when referring to one's own actions, and to use varying intonation and gesture to hold the attention of listeners characterize ghetto language and reinforce the idea of black language as a performing art.

Ghetto talk thus appears to be an artistic medium, which is crafted by street-corner males. Facility in its use brings status, and the talk is for the most part aggressive and directive, embodying the values subsumed under the heading "soul." This creative and adaptive use of language has its roots in an exploitative and separatist situation; it is as old as America's "peculiar institution" and as recent as Robert Beck's *Mama Black Widow* (1969) or Flip Wilson's Thursday night masterpieces. This does not amount to a simplistic glorification of the noble savage; the proposition here is not that we must exalt lower-class, black, urban males, their language and culture. If an assertion is to be ventured it is one that enjoins recognition and study rather than romantic ecstasy.

The recognition that ghetto language is a unique and dynamic medium that proceeds out of a complex culture has telling rami-

10 Abrahams, p. 138.

fications. First, it necessitates a shift in the academic perspective from the deracination or uprooting of a group of people to the anthropologically justifiable process of acculturation. In the past, when black Americans have been considered men at all, they have been considered what the historian Kenneth Stampp calls "white men in black face"; heretofore, whatever roots the black man possessed were stunted by academic fervor in an attempt to graft civilization upon him. It seemed inconceivable to the learned that, as John Anderson Cassandra phrases it: "you treat me like a mule and I came out like a man"—unbelievable that three-fifths of a man could produce and live a culture. That which was different or unique in the black experience, therefore, was simply eradicated, exploited for profit, or fitted into models designed for other lower-class or minority cultures.

In academic communities across the nation this has resulted in "summer high schools," "transition programs," or "upward bound" organizations staffed with white instructors ready to eradicate those last polka dots on an otherwise white student by implementing a curriculum of the best that has been thought and known in the white world. And the programs are indeed transitional; they show the black student what he will find in his fall-term classrooms. Like other institutions in America, the academic community has made claims of pluralism, but whatever cultural diversity it has achieved has not included the black American, whose culture remains excluded for fairly obvious reasons. Until recently, few academicians—which, given the state of American universities, means white academicians—were willing to view the history of black American culture as a culture, "a whole way of life" separate and distinct from other whole ways of life. This means that one often heard urbane statements about the cultural diversity of American universities that might have come directly from John Henry Newman's learned work, but, paradoxically, when one noted the American university's handling of black American culture, one saw not acculturation and diversity but deracination. And the blunt truth is that this situation continues to exist.

How could a university instructor expect a student who can deliver the following lines to listen contentedly while he is tutored in language skills?

I fucked your mama
Till she went blind.
Her breath smells bad,
But she sure can grind.

I fucked your mama
For a solid hour.
Baby came out
Screaming, Black Power.

Elephant and the Baboon
Learning to screw,
Baby came out looking
Like Spiro Agnew.

Rap Brown's evaluation of the situation seems apt: "And the teacher expected me to sit up in class and study poetry after I could run down shit like that? If anybody needed to study poetry, she needed to study mine. We played the Dozens for recreation, like white folks play Scrabble."[11] The words "she needed to study mine" resound, for that is precisely what the university needs to do. One of the saddest losses to academics has been a neglect of the fruits to be derived from the singular black culture that had its origins in American life; sadder still has been the plight of representatives of that culture, who have been prodded and hoed but seldom cultivated to the benefit of the entire academic community. If the vitality, the new modes of perception, and the altered perspectives that accompany the acculturative process are to enter the ken of the learned, academicians must first acknowledge that "there are no exceptions to the anthropological law that all groups have a culture."[12]

If this premise is granted, the consequences are great. For example, if black ghetto culture constitutes a *specific* culture and not a way of life oriented and determined externally, then American policies will have to change. Heretofore, policymakers assumed that all blacks were merely white men in black face and that relief programs with a middle-class orientation—more money, more jobs, and more color television sets—would alleviate the social problems occasioned by the black ghetto's existence.

11 H. Rapp Brown, *Die Nigger Die!* (New York, 1969), p. 26.
12 Blauner, p. 120.

However, we now know that ghetto culture is a distinctive and self-generating way of life, and the only hope for the alleviation of its problems lies in a thorough understanding of its history and its modes of expression.

A specific area in today's academic situation attests both the importance and the misdirection of the recent discoveries concerning black American culture. In colleges and universities throughout America, black studies programs are being planned and instituted in accord with ideals that are largely middle class. These programs typically require proficiency in one of the "accepted" disciplines, a brief exposure to black American history and literature, and, in some cases, a thesis to be written during the senior year. Such programs are only white academics in black face since the students are seldom exposed to the true contemporary locus of black American culture—the black ghetto and its language.

In black American literature courses, for example, Chester Himes, one of the most "cultured" writers the black experience has produced, is usually omitted. Again, Sandy in Langston Hughes's *Not without Laughter* is normally interpreted as a somewhat pitiable figure since his household lacks a stable and aspiring father; most critics fail to realize that Sandy gains more essential wisdom during his days as a shoeshine boy in a black barber shop and as a frequenter of the black pool hall than most children gain in a lifetime. *The Autobiography of Malcolm X* is too often compared solely with *The Autobiography of Benjamin Franklin*, and the dimensions that result from a recognition of Malcolm as a man-of-words are lost.

In order to come to terms with black American literature, one has to recognize it as the product of a culture that places high value on oral presentation. From the unrecorded moment when a "black and unknown" bard sang of stealing away, down to Nikki Giovanni's "Nikki-Rosa," black artists have relied on intonation, inflection, and the distinctive connotations of their language to convey their meanings. Barred from reading and writing by the laws of the land, black American slaves had to devise means of communication (and hence of cultural expression) independent of formal, written presentation, and the most obvious means for the slaves—as for "unsophisticated" folk throughout world history—were the folk song and the folk tale.

The oral forms of the black slave, however, differed from those of other folk cultures; they were, for the most part, indigenous, group forms. While Achilleus, Beowulf, and Davy Crockett capture the heroic virtues of their respective cultures and proclaim them in a public manner, the virtues of black folk heroes are often only implied in the songs and tales. In short, there is a psychical component in black animal tales, trickster slave tales, spirituals, work songs, and sermons that was grasped only by the slave community.

Most early white commentators on black American folklore, finding the language a pidginized English and the tales amusing, decided that the slaves were generally a primitive, poetic, and contented group.[13] Other commentators looked at black American spirituals and found that the vocabulary was that of white Protestantism; it was but a short step to the assumption that black slaves had borrowed their songs from white camp meetings. The failure of early commentators (and that of many since their time) was one of preconception. Predisposed by the tracts of their times (from the 1830s on, according to Mina Davis Caulfield),[14] which portrayed blacks as sambo personalities, commentators could not believe that black folklore was a vital element in a process of culture-building, an element that included not only poetry and amusement but also a private statement of survival values. That the songs and tales of the black man could be antithetical to the oppressive mainstream values was inconceivable to most. Yet, we know that for a slave to "steal away" could not have been beneficial to the economy of his plantation, and we can be certain that Brer Rabbit, for the slaves, was composed of the same heroic material (the same mastery of disguise and deportment) that enabled Frederick Douglass to escape from the eastern shore of Maryland.

There is an infrastructure, an inner core of pressure that pushes at the linguistic surface of even the simplest black folk song or tale, and it is this structure or pressure that gives the most important symbolic value not only to black American folklore

[13] See *The Negro and His Folklore in Nineteenth-Century Periodicals,* ed. Bruce Jackson (Austin, 1967).

[14] Mina Davis Caulfield, "Slavery and the Origins of Black Culture: Elkins Revisited," in *Americans from Africa,* ed. Peter I. Rose (New York, 1970), pp. 186–87.

but also to the works of the consciously literary black tradition. What, for example, is Bigger Thomas if not a more complex version of the badman hero seen in "Stackolee" or "Bad Man"? What is Ellison's protagonist if not a version of the apparently naive trickster seen in "Why Br'Gator's Hide Is So Horny" or "A Laugh That Meant Freedom"?[15] Beyond the obvious categories and the standard folkloristic and literary features of black folklore and literature, however, there is a world of meaning that one can grasp only through an understanding of the distinctiveness of black American language. The language is *sui generis* because it proceeds from a unique culture that is responsible for the pressure which carries its linguistic artifacts beyond formal, white, academic categories. When William Wells Brown manifested a great reluctance to part with his first name for the sake of his Quaker rescuer, when the doctors in Ellison's surrealistic hospital repeated "What is your name?", *ad nauseum*, when James Baldwin proclaimed that "nobody knows my name," and when Malcolm Little changed his name to Malcolm X, this pressure was at work.[16] The simple English word *name* has an awesome significance for black American culture that it can never possess for another culture; the quest for being and identity that begins in a nameless and uncertain void exerts a pressure on the word *name* that can be understood only when one understands black American culture. The culture from which it grows helps to elucidate the language, and, paradoxically, one of the surest ways of understanding the culture is through its linguistic artifacts. Beginning, therefore, with ghetto language and its implications, we are drawn back through the history of a culture and made aware of the distinctiveness of its literature.

This discussion does not constitute an excursus; it suggests that new dimensions and new methodologies are inevitable results of an effective study of black American culture. Black studies programs, therefore, should not be formulated to provide black materials for existing white molds; the programs should be designed to insure a transference of cultural traits between the

---

[15] These tales and ballads appear in *The Book of Negro Folklore*, ed. Arna Bontemps and Langston Hughes (New York, 1958).

[16] These instances of the theme are drawn from *Narrative of William Wells Brown, Invisible Man, Nobody Knows My Name*, and the *Autobiography of Malcolm X*, respectively.

white culture that has been the focus of American universities since their inception and a dynamic black culture that the universities have excluded. In order to fulfill its role as an inculcational institution, the American university will have to emphasize a bicultural experience—one composed of the separate and unique cultures predominant in this country. There are no easy mechanisms for bringing this about, and new methodologies are not likely to spring forth like Athena from the brow of Zeus, or fully developed and competent like Henry "Box" Brown on his arrival in the North. The only methodology currently available is a timeless one: a recognition of ignorance and an attempt to gain wisdom.

The scholar cannot pass his responsibilities on to the black studies program; he must become bilingual and bicultural in order to perform his task of cultural transmission. And since "cultural elements are capable of adoption only in a form which has bearing on the adaptation of the group,"[17] the scholar who understands the group in which the black American student has his genesis is more likely to provide forms that will insure acculturation. In short, a true black studies program is not a limited enterprise; it starts with black language and culture (which are accessible in the black ghettos of every major American city) and is capable of generating new pedagogical methods, new dimensions in our critical perspective, and new methodologies for the study of all disciplines. In the area of black studies, therefore, recent discoveries in black culture could have far-reaching and beneficial effects, and it is lamentable that we recognize this and still have to acknowledge that what is often passed off today as a black studies program no more deserves that title than most American universities deserve to be called culturally pluralistic institutions.

And so we return to Baldwin's John Grimes, a ghetto male, who, like so many of his culture, finds innovative means of adjusting to an exploitative environment and stirring means of articulating that adjustment. But when John speaks the last words of the novel—"I'm ready. I'm coming. I'm on my way."— will we be listening, or shucking and jiving?

[17] Caulfield, p. 183.

VIII   Racial Wisdom and
Richard Wright's *Native Son*

I

I T IS impossible to comprehend the process of transcribing
cultural values without an understanding of the changes
that have characterized both the culture as a whole and the
lives of its individual transcribers. In the case of black American
culture the principal shift was from a rural to an urban environment; similarly, the patterns in the life of Richard Wright
modulated from Mississippi youth to Parisian manhood. Black
American literature has a human immediacy and a pointed
relevance which are obscured by the overingenious methods of
the New Criticism, or any other school that attempts to talk of
works of art as though they had no creators or of sociohistorical
factors as though they did not filter through the lives of individual human beings. The study of biography, in the case of Richard
Wright and his most famous novel, *Native Son*, is a necessity, for
the autobiographical element is strong in all of Wright's work,
and it is impossible to understand the aspirations, turnings, and
contradictions of his work without some understanding of his
life.

Diversity and complexity were present from the outset in the
fair-skinned, literate and retiring Ellen Wilson and the powerful, dark, and uneducated sharecropper from Mississippi's Upper
Delta, Nathan Wright, who were married in 1907. A year later,
on September 4, when Nathan found himself deeper in debt to
the plantation owner who furnished the essentials of his tenancy,
Richard Wright was born. His birthplace was Natchez, but his
life was more influenced by his early migrations than by any one
specific place. According to Blyden Jackson, the character of
Wright's life proceeded from the masses of America's "Black
Belt," a dense Southern body that has thinned since the turn of

the century and become the mass of America's urban ghettos.[1]
During his first nineteen years, Wright was nurtured on the values, modes of adaptation, patterns of social and religious organization, bitterness, aspirations, and violence of the Southern
black American folk. And during these years he moved from
Natchez to Memphis, from Memphis to Jackson, from Jackson
to Elaine, Arkansas, and from Elaine back to Jackson, where he
completed the ninth grade of Smith-Robertson Public School
in 1925. The next move was to Memphis, and here the young boy
worked until he had earned enough money to depart from the
southern black folk and join the northern in the Promised
Land of the American city. It is a dynamic, flowing pattern,
which Wright reduced to its essentials in *Black Boy*, an autobiography published in 1945.

Hunger, fear, a father who deserted the family, the violence
of whites who killed one of his uncles in order to take over his
property, the malignity of a sporting "professor" who was court-
ing his aunt and who murdered a white woman with whom he
was having an affair and burned the house that contained her
lifeless body—these were but a few of the grim elements of
Wright's early life. There was also the domineering Uncle Tom
who once advanced on his young relative with a switch:

"I've got a razor in each hand!" I warned in a low, charged voice.
"If you touch me, I'll cut you, so help me God!"
He paused, staring at my lifted hands in the dawning light of
morning. I held a sharp blue-edge of steel tightly between thumb and
forefinger of each fist.
"My God," he gasped.[2]

Violence was omnipresent: there were beatings by whites, black
women raped, black men ("bad niggers") fighting back, some of
them castrated and lynched. Squalor, fanaticism, and fear characterized the decaying black tenements of southern cities. And a
grandmother's overzealous devotion to the Seventh-Day Advent-
ist Church left as much of an imprint on Wright's early years as
the custom-ridden relations between black men and white wom-

[1] Blyden Jackson, "Richard Wright: Black Boy from America's Black Belt
and Urban Ghettos," *CLA Journal*, XII (June, 1969), 287–309.
[2] Richard Wright, *Black Boy* (New York, 1963), p. 175. All citations in my
text refer to this edition.

en. The primary element of his life, however, and of all black
lives in America, in the words of Stephen Henderson, was
"survival motion."[3]

The principal of Smith-Robertson considered Wright an
outstanding student, and the editor of Jackson's *Southern Reg-
ister* accepted a melodramatic short story, "The Voodoo of Hell's
Half-Acre," in 1924 and encouraged the author to continue
writing; these were two bright spots in a world of leanness and
neglect. The young man left the South, however, with more than
he conceived. From his first screams in a sharecropper's cabin
to his stealthy departure by night from Jackson, he had been im-
mersed in the culture of the black American folk; he rode a night
train to Chicago, a man imbued with the concepts, skills, arts,
and institutions of America's black folk population.

The northern phase of Wright's life did nothing toward the
deculturation of the young man of twenty who arrived in Chicago on a chill December day and made his way to an enclave of
black urban culture. His experiences in Chicago and New York
for the next twenty years simply reinforced the fundamental
attitudes and assumptions he had acquired in the South. Here in
the North he also found hunger, "Negro jobs," excessive black
population density, intra- and interracial violence, decaying tenements, resentful blacks, and prejudiced whites. The environment
altered the modes of adaptation of the folk, but the primary goal
and driving impetus of black life was the same as in the South—
survival, by any means necessary.

Of course, there is no need to minimize the genuine broaden-
ing that Wright underwent in social, intellectual, artistic, and
economic spheres during the thirties and forties. The process of
self-education that he had begun while working for an optical
firm in Memphis continued when he moved to Chicago. Here
he did not have to borrow a white man's library card or forge a
note saying, "Dear Madam: Will you please let this nigger boy
have some books by H. L. Mencken?"[4] but he did have to move

3 Stephen E. Henderson, " 'Survival Motion': A Study of the Black Writer and
the Black Revolution in America," in *The Militant Black Writer in Africa and
the United States*, by Mercer Cook and Stephen E. Henderson, (Madison, Wis.,
1969), pp. 63–129.
4 Wright, *Black Boy*, p. 270.

beyond the boundaries of his own ghetto environment in order to obtain the type of intellectual stimulation he desired. The John Reed Club of Chicago (an organization of radical artists and writers) and the Communist party of America seemed to promise this stimulation. The John Reed Clubs were nationally organized by the Communist party in 1932, and by March of the following year Wright was not only executive secretary of the Chicago branch, but also an official member of the party. The writers associated with these clubs throughout the country were some of the most noted in white and black American literature—John Dos Passos, Langston Hughes, Theodore Dreiser, Malcolm Cowley, and others. Under the auspices and tutelege of the John Reed Club and the party, Wright produced poetry, essays, and fiction dedicated to the melioration of world social conditions. His intellectual and social vision expanded to include the lowly and oppressed from all points of the compass, and he genuinely believed (and there are "many thousands gone" who did likewise) that the Communist party was committed to the cause of civil rights for the black man in America.

The Communist experience for Wright, however, was more than dedication and social vision. Early in his encounters with the party, he felt that he could enjoy warm and sincere human relationships for the first time in his life. Jan Wittenberger (surely the model for Jan Erlone in *Native Son*), who recruited Wright for the John Reed Club, was undoubtedly the person who reinforced this view of human relations in the party.

Considering his life as a whole, one can see that communism was, in fact, an ideology that fit Wright's fundamental cultural assumptions rather than a political camp for which he had to remold his life and values. A communal or collectivistic ethos has always characterized black culture in America, distinguishing it unequivocally from white American culture. The latter endorses individualism and self-help as roads to advancement, but black Americans have long known (as David Walker's *Appeal* [1829] and Henry Highland Garnet's "Address to the Slaves of the United States" [1843] demonstrate) that there can be no advancement of the black individual until the social, economic, and political codes of society have been altered in a manner that makes possible the upward mobility of the entire body of black

Americans. Seldom, for all too patent reasons, have black Americans viewed society as a protective arena in which the individual can work out his own destiny.

It is essential to understand the basis in black culture for Wright's "natural allegiance" to the Communist party. This helps to elucidate the theme and structure of both *Uncle Tom's Children* and *Native Son* to a greater degree than does a critical perspective grounded in Marxist ideology. The group which provided (in Sainte-Beuve's phrase) "all the maturing and value" for Richard Wright, also suggested the strategies of survival and conditioned the world view that Wright set forth in literature. In one of the most ideological stories in *Uncle Tom's Children*, "Fire and Cloud," it is not communism that wins the day for Reverend Taylor and his congregation; it is rather a fused strength based on black religion and reinforced by the belief that not God but "the black people" should receive one's sincerest tributes.[5] In the other stories of *Uncle Tom's Children*, this same sense of fused strength is evident; there is the same affirmation of the positive good to be derived from the unification of black people to overcome their oppressors. The theme of the volume, that "freedom belongs to the strong," certainly implies that Wright believed a united black community stabilized by shared cultural assumptions had the greatest chance of achieving freedom.

In *Native Son*, Bigger Thomas dreams of a strong black man who will emerge to unite the mass of black people. The fulfillment of his dream, of course, is Bigger himself. He accepts the whole way of life that is his culture, and at the end of the novel he emerges as the same type of existential character we see in autobiographical accounts of black American slaves. A case in point is the *Narrative of William Wells Brown, a Fugitive Slave.* One of the most memorable sequences in this narrative records the stages of Brown's physical and psychological movement away from his owners and across the state of Ohio to freedom. Having reclaimed the name of "William," which his master took from him, and having repudiated "trust" and "honor" as they have been defined by his master ("Servants, obey your masters"), he sits cold and alone by a makeshift fire, eating stolen ears of corn,

5 Richard Wright, *Uncle Tom's Children* (New York, 1963), p. 156.

but feeling "all right." Bigger's movement from bondage to freedom follows the same course: he repudiates white American culture, affirms the black survival values of timely trickery and
militant resistance, and serves as a model hero—a strong man
getting stronger, to use Sterling Brown's words—for all readers
of *Native Son* who possess the culture which provided maturation
and value for Richard Wright.

An important distinction must be made between the works of
Richard Wright and the works of the Proletarian School of the
thirties and forties. While it is true that Wright was influenced
by the naturalism and the polemical concerns of contemporary
writers, it is also true that his use of naturalism was not the
ideologically and literarily self-conscious choice made by such
men as John Dos Passos, Mike Gold, and John Steinback. Comparing Wright's life with that of almost any of Emile Zola's protagonists, one immediately recognizes the similarity. Wright's
existence in the Black Belt and in the urban ghettos of America
was one in which events seemed predetermined by heredity (the
simple fact of melanin), and the environment seemed under
divine injunction to destroy. Wright's choice of communism on
an ideological plane and his adoption of naturalism on a literary
plane were, in part, culturally determined, and they led to works
that mark a high point in the black American literary tradition.
One cannot apply critical censures designed for American proletarian literature to Wright's work without just reflection. The
following statement by Nathan Scott serves to illustrate:

And, however robust our respect may still be for the Dos Passos of
the *U.S.A.* trilogy or the Steinbeck of *The Grapes of Wrath* or the
Wright of *Native Son*, we find them today to be writers with whom it
is virtually impossible any longer to have a genuinely reciprocal
relation, for the simple fact is that the rhetoric of what once used
to be called "reportage" proves itself, with the passage of time, to be
a language lacking in the kind of amplitude and resonance that
lasts. This may not be the precise judgment which the cunning of
history, in its ultimate justice, will sustain, but it is, at any rate, *ours*.[6]

Without entertaining the "ultimate," it seems apparent that such
a generalized formula is not applicable to Richard Wright.

[6] Nathan A. Scott, Jr., "The Dark and Haunted Tower of Richard Wright," in
Black Expression, ed. Addison Gayle, Jr. (New York, 1969), p. 308.

Wright's most significant niche is scarcely to be found in the Proletarian School.

When his comrades in the Communist party increased his anxieties by ominous hints of purges in Moscow and talk of the fate of "bastard intellectuals" and "incipient Trotskyites" in their midst, Wright realized that he did not belong in the Marxist gallery. In 1937 his "Fire and Cloud" had won *Story* magazine's prize for the best short story of the year; 1939 brought him a Guggenheim fellowship; and in 1940, *Native Son* was chosen as a Book-of-the-Month Club selection and Wright was awarded the Spingarn Medal by the National Association for the Advancement of Colored People. As an established author, Wright asserted his artistic perogatives and was more than miffed when the party criticized *Native Son* for—of all things—its individualism and its failure to portray the black and white masses of America. In the early forties the party also shifted its policies toward the American Negro; no longer was the granting of the rights of full citizenship to black Americans to be a goal. By the end of 1943, therefore, Wright had withdrawn from the party. In 1944 he published "I Tried to Be a Communist," and five years later he contributed a piece to Richard Crossman's *The God That Failed,* a collection of essays reflecting the disenchantment of former communist supporters.

During the early forties Wright had made even more fundamental shifts in his status. In 1940 he married a ballet dancer, whom he divorced after they had spent an extended (but, for Wright, all too "bourgeois") season in Mexico, and in 1941 he married Ellen Poplar, a Polish member of the Communist party in New York. In effect, the dream with which he leaves his readers at the end of *Black Boy* had come true: he had achieved fame and stability as a writer (the earnings from his writings totalled thirty thousand dollars), he had married the woman he loved, and his daughter Julia, born in 1942, was moving into a beautiful and precocious childhood. But living in New York has never been easy for a black man, and when an invitation to visit France was extended by the French government, Wright promptly accepted.

Soon after his return from Paris in 1947, while walking the streets of Greenwich Village one day and marvelling at the abundance of America, he paused before a small store's display, then decided to buy some fruit to take home. While he was making his selection, the Italian owner rushed out of the store and brusquely asked, "Whudda yuh want, boy?" With the question, Wright's feeling of a moment before—"It's like Christmas! Just like Christmas!"—vanished, and once again he was suffering the "old and ancient agonies" at the hands of his white American neighbors. One individual from what Ellison calls "the waves of immigrants who have come later and passed us by" had made Wright acutely aware of his true culture. His white neighbors on Charles Street were not the least bit kinder; on occasions, the word "nigger," spoken distinctly and loudly enough for him to hear, drifted from a group of white gossipers as he climbed the steps to his home. After a short and frustrating stay in the United States, therefore, Wright departed once more for France and never again saw his native land.

The last thirteen years of his life were full ones; they were charged with new experiences, interesting friendships, accolades as well as indifference for his works, hope for an emerging Africa and a dying colonialism, feelings of awe before an advanced technology, interest in French existentialism (which accorded with Wright's modes of interpreting experience), new world leaders, and his own possessive involvement with his family— the brilliant Julia, energetic Rachel (a second daughter, born in 1949), and devoted Ellen. In "Alas, Poor Richard," James Baldwin characterizes Wright's Paris years as a time of disillusionment and surliness, but one does not receive the same impression from Constance Webb's *Richard Wright.*[7] An understanding of Baldwin's Oedipal rage and unhappiness because Wright, his artistic *paterfamilias,* could not be easily purged from his psyche somehow leads one to place more faith in Miss Webb's assessment.

The works of the last years, from *The Outsider* (a novel, 1953) to *Eight Men* (a collection of short stories prepared for publication in 1960 but published posthumously in 1961), reflect

7 James Baldwin, "Alas, Poor Richard," in *Nobody Knows My Name* (New York, 1968), pp. 146–70; Constance Webb, *Richard Wright, a Biography* (New York, 1968). This work is at present the most definitive biography of Wright; the book is sensitive, intelligent, and well-written. It is one of the few biographical accounts from which the reader receives a genuine feeling for the subject, and I have relied heavily on it. John A. Williams's *The Most Native of Sons* (Garden City, N.Y., 1970) offers a straightforward though more elementary approach to Wright's life.

Wright's attempts to continue his self-education and to order
in some way the swiftly changing world around him. Africa and
Asia seemed to Wright (as they had to W. E. B. Du Bois more
than half a century earlier) to hold both a threat and a promise
for the modern world, and he explored the complexities of the
color line and the new "tragic elite" (leaders of former colonial
territories) in *Black Power*, a report on his visit to the Gold Coast
in 1954, and in *The Color Curtain*, a report on the Asian Ban-
dung Conference in 1956. Spain also was an attractive yet baf-
fling country to Wright, and following his instincts and curiosity
he visited it twice in an attempt to order his reactions; *Pagan
Spain* (1956) was the result. Ever since the Civil War of the
thirties, Spain had proved a fertile subject for contemporary
writers. Wright's own view was charactistically conditioned by
his own background. He understood the mentality of the Spanish peasant, and this, coupled with his knowledge of the social,
theological, and economic patterns of an industrial world, make
Pagan Spain an insightful and provocative book.

The creative works of the last years include *Savage Holiday*
(1954) and *The Long Dream* (1958). Both novels examine the
condition of the contemporary man in an exploitative world, but
neither met with even a mild critical success. In part this cool
reception (indifferent in the case of *Savage Holiday*) was justified. The books are not candidates for rave reviews, and in both
there is a tension between a metaphysical rebellion (which was
much more forceful in Wright's cathartic years of the thirties
and forties than in the early fifties) and a broad, humanistic view
of the Western world. The attempted unity is ambitious and
commendable, but finally the tension is neither sustained nor
resolved in the fine artistic manner displayed in the author's best
fiction. Another novel, *Lawd Today* (begun in 1934 but published posthumously), has done little to enhance his reputation.
The later works, however, are at times exciting, and they deserve more critical attention than they have received from black
and white American critics, who curiously seem to feel that the
end of Wright's artistic life coincides with his departure from
the United States in 1947.

On November 28, 1960, after three days of tests at the Clinique
Chirurgicale Eugéne Gibez in Paris, Richard Wright, like his
most famous protagonist, was feeling "all right." According to

the tests, his health was apparently fine. During the early evening he had read all of the newspapers, but after placing the book that he was reading on the bedside table, he felt a sharp pain and reached for the signal light.

Three minutes later the floor nurse came out of another patient's room, looked up the hallway and saw Richard's light. She walked quietly in her rubber-soled shoes to his room and entered. Richard lay on his back, his head turned toward the door, an apologetic smile on his lips as though to excuse himself for disturbing her. Before he could speak he simply seemed to fall away, his face smoothed of lines. Richard Wright was dead at fifty-two years of age.[8]

Possibly Wright's strange smile had as much to do with the absurdity of dying when he had so many plans as with his feelings toward the nurse. An ambitious, searching, and strong man, his works seldom manifest anything like a Freudian death urge; his protagonists are always committed to a life lived fully and wholly. There are always obstacles in their path, and they are often destroyed as a result of their commitment, but the title of a long work planned shortly before his death captures the mood of his fiction. The proposed title was "Celebration." Wright's works are generally celebrations of life, particularly the complex life lived by black Americans. Wright repeatedly declares that blacks are affirmers: every imaginable pressure has been exerted against them while they have continued to assert the principles of humanity vested in the American Constitution and the Bill of Rights more fully and effectively than any other group on the continent. The native son, in his eyes, could only be the black American. Bigger Thomas's history is the history of black American culture, which coincides precisely with the founding and duration of the United States. From 1619 to the present, black American culture has grown and flourished, and *Native Son* irrefutably demonstrates that Richard Wright was one of its finest artists and most sensitive chroniclers.

II

For thirty years criticism and commentary on *Native Son* have mounted: positive and negative, insightful and absurd, respect-

[8] Webb, p. 399.

ful and racist—the criticism seems to reflect the fundamental
reactions of America to its own history. The aim of the protagonist has been fulfilled: ". . . he wished that he could be an idea
in their minds; that his black face and the image of his smother-
ing Mary and cutting off her head and burning her could hover
before their eyes as a terrible picture of reality which they could
see and feel and yet not destroy."[9] Bigger Thomas struck America's most sensitive nerve; he attacked the white female, its "symbol of beauty" (p. 155). There is little mystery about *Native Son*'s
ability to attract successive generations of American readers; the
great taboo of American culture is shattered in the book, and
human beings, like Ralph Ellison's Mr. Norton in *Invisible Man*,
possess a fateful desire to look upon chaos without being destroyed. It is Trueblood in *Invisible Man*, however, who actually
has vision, and in Wright's novel it is Bigger Thomas. Mr.
Norton remains sightless, and those surrounding Bigger (Mrs.
Dalton and even the sympathetic lawyer, Boris Max) persist in
their blindness.[10]

There is some irony in the fact that critics—black and white—
search the novel's image clusters, dialogue, point of view, ideology, and allusions for the source of its power. Those who have
undertaken such structural safaris have often shared Mr. Norton's and Mrs. Dalton's fate; they have remained blind to one of
the most essential sources of power. Codes restricting the alliance
of blacks and whites in colonial America, a Civil War, anti-
miscegenation laws, thousands of lynchings, the murder of Em-
mett Till—all point to one reason for *Native Son*'s force; these
manifestations of American culture reinforce Bigger's belief that
Mary Dalton and her kin are "the flowers" of American civilization, the symbols of purity and innocence which the country has
sought to protect. A young white female suffocated, decapitated,
and cast into a roaring furnace by a twenty-year-old black man
who glories in his act—this is the image that remains fixed in
the reader's mind. And the image is not merely melodrama or
sensationalism.

Melodramatic and sensational impulses usually proceed from

[9] Richard Wright, *Native Son* (New York, 1966), p. 123. All citations in my text
refer to this edition.
[10] In the Signet edition of *Invisible Man* (New York, 1952), the Norton-
Trueblood encounter covers pp. 46–66.

the exploitative regions of an author's soul; they are composed of clichés, set formulas, and exaggerations designed to manipulate the emotions of the reader. The genesis of *Native Son* goes deeper; the book comes from a region where only truth will suffice, a region into which the unpleasant facts of history intrude for honest scrutiny, a realm where myths and stereotypes dissolve and a genuine folk heritage shines forth. When Bigger forces Mary's body into the flames, his act is no more terrifying than a slave's slapping his white mistress to frighten away an opponent. Bigger's swing of the hatchet to take off Mary's head is no more awesome than the decisive stroke with which Nat Turner took the life of his white mistress. Stackolee's fearful acts, which stop the white sheriff from coming after him, are no less daring than Bigger's resistance to the white mob that comes seeking his life, and Brer Rabbit and the hero of the "John Cycle"—both accomplished tricksters—would have been proud of Bigger's handling of the obtuse detective Britten and the voyeuristic reporters who come to the Dalton home in search of melodrama and sensation.

Bigger's culture is that of the black American race, and he is intelligible as a conscious literary projection of the folk hero who embodies the survival values of a culture. Tales of the trickster animal who overcomes his stronger opponents, of John, the slave who outwits his master, of the "bad nigger" (Shine, Stackolee, Dupree) who rebels against an oppressive system—all of these contribute to an understanding of Wright's protagonist. Tales of pillage and plunder, accounts of black men inflicting pain and humiliation on white women with impunity, and stories of injustices suffered by black Americans are plentiful in black folklore, and a tale such as the following helps to illuminate the perspective of *Native Son*:

In a little Southern town, a mob was fixing to lynch a man when a very dignified old judge appeared. "Don't," he pleaded, "put a blot on this fair community by hasty action. The thing to do," he insisted, "is to give the man a fair trial and then lynch him." [11]

The story is Bigger Thomas's, and if a representative tale from the white-woman genre is considered, the perspective becomes even clearer:

[11] Richard M. Dorson, *American Negro Folktales* (New York, 1970), p. 504.

You take in the South, they always have one strong colored guy on all the plantations. He's given a lot of consideration by the boss— usually he be foreman. Can put two or three of the others in his back pocket.

The story goes on to tell of two such men whose masters arranged for them to fight one another. On the day of the fight, Jim, one of the combatants, in an attempt to frighten John, his adversary, has his boss attach him to an iron chain staked in the ground. But John arrives at the battling grounds, slaps his own boss's wife in the face, and watches Jim run away:

So the loser, Jim's master, had to pay off John's boss the three or four thousand dollars they'd put in a bag. Still, John's boss got mad about his wife being slapped. He asked John, "What was the idea slapping my wife?" "Well, Jim knowed if I slapped a white woman I'd a killed him, so he run." [12]

John's concluding words bring to mind the fate of Bessie Mears. When we combine tales of injustice and white-woman tales with stories of the bad-man hero, the picture is complete. A white sheriff responds to Billy Lyons's mother:

Sheriff said, My name might begin with an *s* and end with an *f*, But if you want that bad Stackolee you got to get him yourself.

Black folklore includes countless examples of strong black men giving "a faint, wry, bitter smile," or the final, destructive thrust to the revered symbols of white America, and Bigger Thomas's act is simply a continuation of this heritage.

Why, then, have Bigger's character and action, which are built of so many traditional elements, aroused such concern? The answer is not far to seek. Genuine black folklore has seldom been considered valid literary or historical evidence by our cultural custodians. The arts of the black American folk (rural and urban) have been largely ignored, caricatured, or exploited by white America. Black music was transformed into the distorted croons of the minstrel tradition. The forceful idioms of black folk speech were converted into the muddled syntax and thick-lipped jargon of "Negro jokes." Bessie Smith and Louis Armstrong wailing and transcending in the cabarets of Harlem became Paul Whiteman and George Gershwin harmonizing in theatres downtown.

[12] *Ibid.,* pp. 134–35.

In short, the art of black folk culture (like the art of other American subcultures, such as the Irish, Italian, and Jewish) has been adjusted to suit the needs of white America—to reinforce stereotypes and sometimes even to justify the victimization of the black American. America at large has seldom taken an honest look at its black citizenry.

Since black Americans were kept illiterate by the laws of the land during much of their history, they could not challenge the general American view of the black man in poetry or prose. And when black writers did take pen in hand, polemical demands (the need to castigate slavery and caste in America) and the bare formal requirements of their craft exerted pressures that relegated the true folk heritage to a somewhat minor role. This does not mean that the folk heritage was forgotten; James Weldon Johnson's *The Autobiography of an Ex-Colored Man*, Jean Toomer's *Cane*, Langston Hughes's *Not without Laughter*, and Arna Bontemps's *Black Thunder* all rely on the folk experience. But Richard Wright's *Native Son* was the first black novel that captured its full scope and dimension.

Wright's message to America was that black Americans are a unique people who have produced heroes who hate and wish to destroy those contrived symbols of white culture that insure our victimization. Bigger says to his lawyer:

"What I killed for must've been good! . . . It must have been good! When a man kills, it's for something. . . . I didn't know I was really alive in this world until I felt things hard enough to kill for 'em. . . . It's the truth, Mr. Max. I can say it now, 'cause I'm going to die. I know what I'm saying real good and I know how it sounds. But I'm all right. I feel all right when I look at it that way. . . ."[13]

The voices of David Walker, Nat Turner, Frederick Douglass, Martin Delaney, and a dishevelled group of black forced laborers singing "Lookin' fer Jimbo / Don' say nothin' / Go 'head Jimbo / Don' say nothin' " resound through Bigger's words.[14] The message is simple: reverberating through black folk culture it says, "Mean mean mean to be free."[15] Wright's theme and his hero

---

[13] *Native Son*, p. 392; Wright's ellipses.
[14] Quoted from *The Book of Negro Folklore*, ed. Arna Bontemps and Langston Hughes (New York, 1958), "Hyah Come de Cap'm," p. 405.
[15] Robert Hayden, "Runagate Runagate," in *Selected Poems* (New York, 1966), p. 77.

were drawn from the folk history to which he was heir. America's attraction to *Native Son* has been the response of the curious to the unknown, the guilty to the reason for guilt, the deceitful to exposure, the sympathetic to the oppressed, the learned to new evidence, and the perceptive to works of genius. No cultural historian (a role that Wright self-consciously assumed the year following *Native Son* in *Twelve Million Black Voices: A Folk History of the Negro in the United States*) could have hoped to evoke more response than *Native Son* did.

Irving Howe has presented a just assessment of Wright's achievement: "The day *Native Son* appeared, American culture was changed forever. No matter how much qualifying the book might later need, it made impossible a repetition of the old lies."[16] Wright brought to consummation the black artist's struggle to express a folk heritage in unequivocal terms; neither polemical demands nor the requirements of his craft distorted his portrayal of the conditions of blackness in America. In short, *Native Son* accomplished the task begun by the black intelligentsia (including Paul Laurence Dunbar, Charles Chesnutt, James Weldon Johnson, and W. E. B. Du Bois) at the turn of the century; Wright successfully translated the values of an oral tradition into written form. And the reading public's overwhelming reaction to his novel has been one of praise and discovery, shock and genuine appreciation; in the midst of white America is a culture—a whole way of life—with values in many ways antithetical to those of the larger society, values symbolized by and epitomized in a five-foot, nine-inch black man following the example of his folk predecessors by pushing a cherished white symbol into oblivion.

III

To view Wright as a historian of black folk culture, however, raises several problems for the study of *Native Son*. In "How 'Bigger' Was Born" (1940) and again in *Black Boy*, the author seems to deny (or, at least, to disregard) the life-enhancing aspects of black American culture. In "How 'Bigger' Was Born," he im-

16 Irving Howe, "Black Boys and Native Sons," in *A World More Attractive* (New York, 1963), pp. 100–101.

plies that his hero has no integral relation to black folk culture: "First, through some quirk of circumstance, he had become estranged from the religion and the folk culture of his race." [17] This statement makes one recall the conclusions about Coleridge reached by John Livingston Lowes, who after searching many possible sources of the poet's creative works was forced to admit that he could not determine precisely how these sources were transmuted into art. [18] Likewise, the manner in which Wright's experiences were transmuted into art remains unexplained even by himself. When Wright speaks of Bigger's estrangement from black folk culture and religion there is a high degree of critical myopia involved; he reduces folk culture to little more than folk religion. Hence, in *Native Son*, Bigger is estranged from Mrs. Thomas and Reverend Hammond (her minister), who embody the author's perception of his own folk religion. Wright knew that black folk culture was more than otherworldly hymns and humble Hebraism, but in an attempt to explain the genesis of *Native Son* he did not reveal his broader wisdom.

A religious, passive, escapist way of life is presented as the essence of black American culture in "How 'Bigger' Was Born." Nevertheless, in *Native Son* Wright adopted several fully developed strategies from black folk culture that have little to do with humble passivity. From his killing of a rat in the first scene of the novel until his last, bitter smile to his retreating lawyer, Bigger Thomas acts as the eternal man in revolt, a type of devil or badman hero who attempts to subvert society by refusing to heed its dictates. The burning of Mary Dalton's body and the premeditated murder of Bessie Mears are clearly the acts of a strong, Satanic figure determined, at whatever cost, to have his freedom. The moment he adopts a mask of innocence, subserviance, and stupidity to allay the suspicions of detective Britten and the newspaper reporters, Bigger plays the role of the trickster. These activist strategies are quite as important as religion to black American folk culture. "How 'Bigger' Was Born" is an elucidating essay, but ultimately it tells us more about Wright's interpretation of *Native Son* than about the mysteries of the

[17] Richard Wright, "How 'Bigger' Was Born," *Saturday Review*, June 1, 1940, p. 4.

[18] John Livingston Lowes, *The Road to Xanadu: A Study in the Ways of the Imagination* (New York, 1927).

novel's creation. The author did not miss the mark in his attempt
to create an appropriate representative of black folk culture, but
his interpretation of his own paradigmatic creation is simply
too narrow. There is, furthermore, a similar narrowness in
Black Boy.

Innumerable passages in Wright's autobiography give a sense
of black communality, a sense of fused strength, yet the narrator
denies the presence of such meaningful relations in the micro-
cosm that he sets before the reader. There is an almost querulous
insistence that the narrator's is the only sensitive, artistic, struggling soul in this world. In its projection of a creative soul out of
harmony with an oppressive environment, *Black Boy* is generi-
cally akin to the slave narratives, but there is more to it. In essence, Wright's attempt at a recovery of self is more a creative
than an analytical act. Regarding his southern upbringing from
the perspective of a successful author, Wright's memory exer-
cised a meet selectivity; out of terror, illiteracy, and oppression
emerges the young, gifted, black artist. The picture is as stirring
as the autobiographer desired, for he was not reluctant to employ
folk and fictional incidents in *Black Boy* for the creation of effects. Moreover, he never allows fully delineated tenderness or
sentiment to distort the informing purpose of the book—to demonstrate how Richard Wright, the author, was formed. In this
context, Wright's much-debated statements about "the essential
bleakness of black life in America" come as no surprise. It would
be virtually impossible to present a portrait of the *struggling*
artist that delineated his culture as one that provided most of the
essential elements an artist requires. The struggle for fulfillment
would then become more an alternative than a necessity.

If we are to consider him the chronicler of his time, Wright's
parenthetical statements about "the strange absence of real kindness" and "the cultural barrenness of black life" merit our concern. The following paragraph is representative:

Whenever I thought of the essential bleakness of black life in America, I knew that Negroes had never been allowed to catch the full
spirit of Western Civilization, that they lived somehow in it but not
of it. And when I brooded upon the cultural barrenness of black
life, I wondered if clean, positive tenderness, love, honor, loyalty, and
the capacity to remember were native with man. I asked myself if

these human qualities were not fostered, won, struggled and suffered for, presented in ritual form from one generation to another.[19]

Ralph Ellison regards this passage as an affirmation of black culture. Wright, according to Ellison, is pointing out that ". . . Negro sensibility is socially and historically conditioned; that Western Culture must be won, confronted like the animal in a Spanish bullfight, dominated by the red shawl of codified experience and brought heaving to its knees."[20] Dan McCall, on the other hand, feels that the passage is based on Wright's realization of the effects produced by "the terrible cultural bind of the South," which transforms the pain and desire of black life into intraracial violence. Moreover, he feels that the statement is part of the author's attempt to "find a meaning" in the bleakness, terror, lack of kindness, and violence of black life.[21]

Both critics provide useful explications, but neither seems to realize how fully Wright's perception of his relationship to the objective world (the world that had adjudged *Native Son* and its author just claimants to greatness) conditioned the writing of *Black Boy.* The reception of *Native Son* gave Wright the confidence he needed to deal with a world he viewed as tempting, fragmented, and alienating; in *Black Boy,* the intended message is one of transcendence, and in order to drive home its full significance, the author allows monochromatic or unrelieved barrenness to act as scrim and underpinning for the stage on which his narrator acts out his ascent. The total effect of *Black Boy* is magnificent; we bestow kudos where the autobiographer intends, on the hard-earned rise of Richard Wright to eminence.

Once again, however, we see the same type of paradox that confronts the reader of "How 'Bigger' Was Born." It must be kept in mind that a transcendent Richard Wright—an author who had repeatedly employed the communality, modes of adaptation, and intraracial hostility of black culture as subjects for his fiction—tells the reader of a sterile culture that can scarcely be expected to produce such an author. In short, Wright's position

---

[19] *Black Boy*, p. 45. Wright's entire statement is parenthetical and occurs at the beginning of chapter two.

[20] Ralph Ellison, "Richard Wright's Blues," in *Shadow and Act* (New York, 1966), p. 103.

[21] Dan McCall, *The Example of Richard Wright* (New York, 1969), pp. 118–19.

as some readers view it (those observers who perceive him objectively as a writer whose genius was brought to maturity by the group in which he had his genesis) is a tribute to the vitality and creativity of black culture. His position as he perceived it, however, was an altogether different thing, since he regarded himself as both subject and object. And in considering the subject of *Black Boy* he was somewhat myopic; he was unable to see his developed self as sensitive readers can. His pejorative comments on black American culture, therefore, are balanced by the reader's understanding of what Wright sought to achieve, and the fact that he chose to write what Roy Pascal designates "the story of a calling" implies an affirmation of black American culture's ability to produce outstanding authors.[22]

Impulses arising from Wright's culture conditioned his propensity for other realms of experience and influenced his definition of an authorial relationship to them. Bigger Thomas's final stance in *Native Son*, for example, is as existential as Cross Damon's primary stance in *The Outsider*. Yet it was not Wright's contact with Jean Paul Sartre and Simone de Beauvoir that shaped his existential view. The fundamental conditions of black life in America led him to see that a priori moral values could scarcely be operating in the great scheme of events; the quest for value in *Native Son* and *The Outsider*, therefore, does not extend beyond the choices of an individual man with his mind "set on freedom." In the same vein, Wright states in *Black Boy* that his choice of literary mode was not the result of overintellectualization or excessive brooding on white Western culture: "All my life had shaped me for the realism, the naturalism of the modern novel, and I could not read enough of them" (p. 274). Black life in America, which is both existential and communal, was thoroughly naturalistic for Richard Wright.

Wright sought means to order the seeming chaos of the black situation. But that chaos and the means, values, and strategies that black Americans have employed to deal with it were always integral parts of his outlook. In his first novel, he gazed steadily on the face of chaos and created a successful and enduring work, and if one holds *Native Son* alone in evidence, one must agree with Hugh Gloster that Wright, ". . . above all other American

---

[22] Roy Pascall, *Design and Truth in Autobiography* (Cambridge, Mass., 1960).

novelists, is the sensitive painter and perspicacious spokesman of the inarticulate black millions of this country."[23] In "Blueprint for Negro Literature" (published in *New Challenge*, 1937), Wright himself wrote:

It was . . . in a folklore moulded out of rigorous and inhuman conditions of life that the Negro achieved his most indigenous expression. Blues, spirituals, and folk tales recounted from mouth to mouth, the whispered words of a black mother to her black daughter on the ways of men, the confidential wisdom of a black father to his black son, the swapping of sex experiences on street corners from boy to boy in the deepest vernacular, work songs sung under blazing suns, all these formed the channels through which the racial wisdom flowed.[24]

In recording his experiences as an orderly in a Chicago hospital in 1931, Wright tells of assisting as doctors sedated experimental dogs, stuck scalpels down their throats, and slit their vocal cords so that they would not disturb the patients. The awakened dogs, who lifted their eyes to the ceiling and attempted to cry, became for Wright symbols of silent human suffering. Wright's statement in "Blueprint" merges with his experiences in the Chicago hospital, to give a very special impact to Gloster's assessment of the achievement of *Native Son*. Richard Wright moved beyond silent suffering, far beyond inarticulateness; yet when he created it was in the tone and from the perspective of the "inarticulate" black folk of America. The racial wisdom of an accomplished cultural heritage flows through *Native Son*, one of the most dynamic novels in the black American literary tradition.

[23] Hugh Gloster, *Negro Voices in American Fiction* (Chapel Hill, N. C., 1948).
[24] Richard Wright, "Blueprint for Negro Literature," in *Amistad II* (New York, 1971), p. 6. This is a revised and expanded version of Wright's "Blueprint."

IX Conclusion

"H OLD to the now, the here, through which all future plunges to the past," Stephen Dedalus tells himself as he prepares for an intellectual skirmish with the wits and scholars of Dublin. He forgets this injunction rather quickly, however, and the result is a farfetched interpretation of *Hamlet*. One of the prime virtues of fiction is that it presents imagined situations that we are not compelled to emulate in our own lives. Unlike Stephen, who is destined *ad infinitum* to forget his timely caution, we can hold to the here and now and avoid formulating theories that merely gratify the intellectual fancy. The first step toward such a state is a willingness to entertain all ideas and search out all available evidence.

Our contemporaneity, according to T. S. Eliot, hinges on our historical sense, our awareness of where we have been. In his *Essays in the Philosophy of History* (ed. William Dobbins [Austin, Tex., 1965]), R. G. Collingwood states this same proposition in historiographical terms when he says that the past does not exist as something that can be grasped *in toto* but as something that must be reconstructed from present evidence. Collingwood defines evidence as anything that aids the historian in answering questions about the past. For classicists such as Eliot and Collingwood, James Joyce's thesis that history is a nightmare from which man must awaken would have made little sense.

The problems that have beset black American history, literature, and culture have in fact arisen because too many have been willing to accept history as a nightmare and have refused to allow the appropriate questions to rise to human consciousness. When the hysterical child whimpers "it was a nightmare," he is soothed, comforted, and returned to bed. But when a man asks a pointed question, all the intellectual stops should be pulled and a search for honest and elucidating answers begun. Today, innumerable questions about the past of the black American are being posed, and it will no longer suffice to say "it was a nightmare." It is time to insist that whatever is present, tangible, and helpful in answering these questions be considered valid evidence.

First it must be granted that black American culture constitutes, as do all other cultures, a whole way of life common to a significant group of people. Acceptance of this premise carries the investigator beyond the current neoabolitionist battle in which whites shout that blacks are inferior and blacks, like the protagonist of John A. Williams's *The Man Who Cried I Am*, vehemently insist that they are human. The question of the black man's humanity recedes with the acknowledgment of his culture: passive, bestial victims and sambo personalities are not generally what one has in mind when he speaks of culture as a whole way of life. The goal of an investigation of black American culture is to discover what type of man the black American is and what values and experiences he has articulated that might be useful in one's attempts to make sense of the world.

Even at this point, however, there are choices to be made. Rather than search for new evidence, one can simply accept the time-honored treatises that attempt to define the black man or one can listen to those who have already judged the black man's articulated experiences. For example, it is easier to read Irving Howe's assessment of Richard Wright, James Baldwin, and Ralph Ellison than to search for evidence that will reveal the foundations on which black American authors have built. Furthermore, one who has little knowledge of black American culture (save what he has imbibed from black friends or gleaned from the yellowed pages of U. B. Phillips or the fast-yellowing pages of Stanley Elkins) can read the entire canon of black American literature with contentment, never realizing how much he is missing or—which is more to be lamented—misinterpreting.

Black American folklore; the recurrent themes of black American literature; the works of David Walker, Frederick Douglass, Booker T. Washington, and W. E. B. Du Bois; and an understanding of black America's shift from a rural and agrarian to an urban and industrial setting all come to bear in an examination of Richard Wright. These are the traditional elements on which the life and work of Wright were built, and they constitute new evidence. New evidence does not necessarily mean that which has sprung up overnight or come into the world full-blown: black American folklore has existed since the first slave composed a song or crafted a proverb that dealt with his experiences in a strange land; Walker's *Appeal* first appeared in 1829. The *Appeal* and black folklore are not chronologically new, but seldom have they been analyzed and adjudged valid as historical and literary evidence for ascertaining the nature of black American culture. Likewise, ghettos have existed from time immemorial, but a study of the language and culture of the black ghetto offers new (previously unacknowledged or unanalyzed) evidence that is essential for an informed reading of twentieth-century black American literature.

More than pretentious, it would be incorrect to assert that the foregoing essays are radical in content or design. They are attempts to show the distinctiveness of black American culture and to bring into focus evidence that is essential for the critic of black American literature. Rather than paying dutiful homage to Phillis Wheatley, Jupiter Hammon, Frances Harper and a number of other less skillful early black writers, the essays examine the folklore that Frederick Douglass, David Walker, and their accomplished successors built upon. Rather than attempting to force Richard Wright into the naturalistic and proletarian traditions of white American literature, an attempt is made to discover the prime motivating forces of Wright's life and work. Rather than continuing the argument over the black man's humanity the essays acknowledge at the outset the existence of a separate and distinct culture. Such endeavors are more profitable than attempts to ignore black American culture or efforts to define its literature as the spontaneous overflow of primitive black emotions. Moreover, they are more rewarding than a struggle to force both the literature and the culture into preexistent molds that were not designed to contain them.

Those who seek to ignore, to derogate, or to fit black American literature and culture into the old categories would rather soothe the hysterical child and rock him to a deathlike sleep than answer the questions now rising to the consciousness of men. At this historical moment, a decision to investigate the available evidence can open new approaches to criticism and permit a genuine understanding of black American culture. But if we refuse to hold to the now, the here, through which our future plunges, we—like all who do not study history—are destined to relive it.

Bibliography

Index

A Selected Bibliography
of Criticism of Black American Literature
(Arranged in Chronological Order)

I. Folklore

Abrahams, Roger. "The Changing Concept of the Negro Hero." In *The Golden Log*, ed. Mody C. Boatwright, Wilson M. Hudson, Allen Maxwell, pp. 119–34. Dallas: Southern Methodist University Press, 1962.

Bontemps, Arna, and Langston Hughes, eds. *The Book of Negro Folklore*. New York: Dodd, Mead and Co., 1969.

Botkin, B. A. *Lay My Burden Down: A Folk History of Slavery*. Chicago: University of Chicago Press, 1945.

Brewer, J. Mason. *American Negro Folklore*. Chicago: Quadrangle Books, 1968.

———. *The Word on the Brazos*. Austin, Tex.: University of Texas Press, 1953.

Courlander, Harold. *Negro Folk Music, U.S.A.* New York: Columbia University Press, 1963.

Cuney-Hare, Maud. *Negro Musicians and Their Music*. Washington, D.C.: Associated Publishers, 1936.

Dorson, Richard M. *Negro Folktales in Michigan*. Cambridge, Mass.: Harvard University Press, 1956.

Harris, Joel Chandler. *Uncle Remus, His Songs and His Sayings*. New York: Houghton, Mifflin and Co., 1881.

Hurston, Zora Neale. *Mules and Men*. Philadelphia: J. B. Lippincott, 1935.

Jackson, Bruce, ed. *The Negro and His Folklore in the Nineteenth-Century Periodical*. Austin, Tex.: University of Texas Press, 1967.

Johnson, James Weldon. *The Book of American Negro Spirituals*. New York: Viking Press, 1969.

Krehbiel, H. E. *Afro-American Folksongs*. New York: G. Schirmer, 1914.

Puckett, Newbell Niles. *Folk Beliefs of the Southern Negro*. Chapel Hill, N.C.: University of North Carolina Press, 1926.

Weldon, Fred O., Jr. "Negro Folktale Heroes." In *And Horns on the Toads*, ed., Mody C. Boatwright, Wilson M. Hudson, Allen Maxwell. Dallas: Southern Methodist University Press, 1959.

Wilgus, D. K. "The Negro-White Spirituals." In *Anglo-American Folksong Scholarship since 1898*. New Brunswick, N.J.: Rutgers University Press, 1959.

II. Walker, Douglass, Washington, and Du Bois

Aptheker, Herbert. *"One Continual Cry": David Walker's Appeal to the Colored Citizens of the World (1829–1830): Its Setting and Its Meaning*. New York: Humanities Press, 1965.

Bontemps, Arna. *Frederick Douglass: Slave, Fighter, Freeman*. New York: Alfred Knopf, 1959.

——. Introduction to *Great Slave Narratives*. Boston: Beacon Press, 1969.

Broderick, Francis L. *W. E. B. Du Bois, Negro Leader in a Time of Crisis*. Stanford, Calif.: Stanford University Press, 1959.

Clarke, John Henrik, et al. [the *Freedomways* Editors], eds. *Black Titan: W. E. B. Du Bois*. Boston: Beacon Press, 1970.

Foner, Philip. *Frederick Douglass, a Biography*. New York: Citadel Press, 1964.

——. *The Life and Writings of Frederick Douglass*. 4 vols. New York: International Publishers, 1950–55.

Hawkins, Hugh. *Booker T. Washington and His Critics*. Boston: D. C. Heath, 1962.

Meier, August. *Negro Thought in America, 1880–1915: Racial Ideologies in the Age of Booker T. Washington*. Ann Arbor, Mich.: University of Michigan Press, 1963.

Quarles, Benjamin. *Frederick Douglass*. Washington, D.C.: Associated Publishers, 1948.

Rudwick, Elliott M. *W. E. B. Du Bois: A Study in Minority Group Leadership*. Philadelphia: University of Pennsylvania Press, 1960.

——. *W. E. B. Du Bois, Propagandist of the Negro Protest*. New York: Atheneum, 1969.

Spencer, Samuel R. *Booker T. Washington and the Negro's Place in American Life*. Boston: Little, Brown, 1955.

Thornbrough, Emma Lou. *Booker T. Washington*. Englewood Cliffs, N.J.: Prentice-Hall, 1969.

III. Early Poetry, Fiction, and Criticism

Brawley, Benjamin. *Paul Laurence Dunbar, Poet of His People*. Chapel Hill, N.C.: University of North Carolina Press, 1936.
———. *The Negro in Literature and Art in the United States*. New York: Duffield and Co., 1918. Contains chapters on Dunbar, Chesnutt, and Du Bois and critical material on James Weldon Johnson.
Brown, Sterling. *Negro Poetry and Drama*. New York: Atheneum, 1969.
———. *The Negro in American Fiction*. New York: Atheneum, 1969.
Chesnutt, Helen M. *Charles Waddell Chesnutt: Pioneer of the Color Line*. Chapel Hill, N.C.: University of North Carolina Press, 1952.
Cunningham, Virginia. *Paul Laurence Dunbar and His Song*. New York: Dodd, Mead and Co., 1947.
Lawson, Victor. *Dunbar Critically Examined*. Washington, D.C.: Associated Publishers, 1941.
Loggins, Vernon. *The Negro Author and His Development in America*. New York: Columbia University Press, 1931.
Redding, J. Saunders. *To Make a Poet Black*. Chapel Hill, N. C.: University of North Carolina Press, 1939.
Tate, Ernest Cater. *The Social Implications of the Writings and the Career of James Weldon Johnson*. New York: The American Press, 1968.
Terry, Ellen. *Young Jim: The Early Years of James Weldon Johnson*. New York: Dodd, Mead and Co., 1967.
Thorpe, Earl Endris. *Negro Historians in the United States*. Baton Rouge, La.: Fraternal Press, 1958.

IV. The Harlem Renaissance

Bontemps, Arna. "Harlem in the Twenties." *Opportunity*, LXIII (1966).
———. "The Harlem Renaissance." *Saturday Review*, March 22, 1947.
———. "The Negro Renaissance: Jean Toomer and the Harlem Writers of the 1920's." In *Anger, and Beyond*, ed. Herbert Hill, pp. 20–36. New York: Harper and Row, 1969.

Brawley, Benjamin. *The Negro Genius.* New York: Dodd, Mead and Co., 1937.

Bronz, Stephen H. *Roots of Negro Racial Consciousness, the 1920's: Three Harlem Renaissance Authors.* New York: Libra, 1964.

Clarke, John Henrik, ed. *Harlem: A Community in Transition.* New York: Citadel Press, 1964.

Dickinson, Donald C. *A Bio-Bibliography of Langston Hughes, 1902–1967.* Hamden, Conn.: Archon Books, 1967.

Emanuel, James A. *Langston Hughes.* New York: Twayne, 1967.

Ferguson, Blanche E. *Countee Cullen and the Negro Renaissance.* New York: Dodd, Mead and Co., 1966.

Johnson, James Weldon. *Black Manhattan.* New York: Alfred Knopf, 1930.

Locke, Alain. *Four Negro Poets.* New York: Simon and Schuster, 1927. McKay, Toomer, Cullen, and Hughes.

Munson, Gorham B. "The Significance of Jean Toomer." *Opportunity*, III, 1925.

Redding J. Saunders. "Emergence of the New Negro." In *To Make A Poet Black*, pp. 93–125. Chapel Hill, N.C.: University of North Carolina Press, 1939.

V. The Thirties and Forties

Bone, Robert A. *The Negro Novel in America.* New Haven: Yale University Press, 1958.

Butcher, Margaret J. *The Negro in American Culture.* New York: Alfred Knopf, 1956.

Cruse, Harold. *The Crisis of the Negro Intellectual.* New York: William Morrow, 1967.

Gray, Yohma. "An American Metaphor: The Novels of Richard Wright." Ph.D. dissertation, Yale University, 1967.

Kaiser, Ernest. "The Literature of Harlem." In *Harlem: A Community in Transition*, ed. John Henrik Clarke, pp. 26–41. New York: Citadel Press, 1965.

Locke, Alain. "Harlem: Dark Weather Vane." *Survey Graphic.* August, 1936.

———. "The Negro in American Literature." In *New World Writing*, pp. 18–33. New York: New American Library, 1952.

McKay, Claude. *Harlem: A Negro Metropolis.* New York: E. P. Dutton & Co., 1940.

Margolies, Edward. *Native Sons.* New York: J. B. Lippincott, 1969.

——. *The Art of Richard Wright.* Carbondale, Ill: Southern Illinois University Press, 1969.

Sternsher, Bernard, ed. *The Negro in Depression and War: Prelude to Revolution, 1930–1945.* Chicago: Quadrangle Books, 1969. Contains extremely helpful articles by Leslie Fishel, W. E. B. Du Bois, Mary Bethune, Allan Morrison, Richard Dalfiume, and others.

Webb, Constance. *Richard Wright, a Biography.* New York: G. P. Putnam, 1968.

VI. The Fifties and Sixties

Some of the most interesting critical statements about the black American literature of the past two decades have been made by black writers themselves. James Baldwin, Ralph Ellison, LeRoi Jones, Larry Neal, Julian Mayfield, and Don L. Lee have all made important statements about the task of the black artist. Some of these statements have been excerpted in Addison Gayle's *Black Expression,* and others have appeared in such periodicals as *Phylon, The Journal of Negro History, Black World, Liberator, Freedomways,* and *The Journal of Black Poetry.* All of these sources provide invaluable material for the student of recent black American literature, just as the pages of *Crisis* and *Opportunity* provide invaluable material for the student of early twentieth-century black American literature. The list of works below comprises only a brief, selected bibliography of some of the more helpful items dealing with recent black American literature.

Abramson, Doris E. *Negro Playwrights in the American Theatre: 1925–1959.* New York: Columbia University Press, 1969.

Bone, Robert A. *The Negro Novel in America.* New Haven: Yale University Press, 1958.

Bontemps, Arna. "The New Black Renaissance." *Negro Digest,* XI (November, 1961), 52–58.

Brown, Sterling. "A Century of Negro Portraiture in American Literature." *Massachusetts Review,* VII (1966), 73–96.

Clarke, John Henrik. *Malcolm X: The Man and His Times.* New York: Macmillan Co., 1969.

Cook, Mercer, and Stephen Henderson. *The Militant Black Writer in Africa and the United States.* Madison, Wis.: University of Wisconsin Press, 1969.

Eckman, Fern Marja. *The Furious Passage of James Baldwin.* New York: J. B. Lippincott, 1967.

Ellison, Ralph. "The World and the Jug." In *Shadow and Act* (New York: Random House, 1964), 115–148. This is Ellison's answer to Irving Howe's essay "Black Boys and Native Sons." Howe's essays can be found in *A World More Attractive* (New York: Horizon Press, 1963).

Gayle, Addison, Jr., ed. *Black Expression: Essays by and about Black Americans in the Creative Arts.* New York: Weybright and Talley, 1969.

Gross, Seymour L., and John Edward Hardy, eds. *Images of the Negro in American Literature.* Chicago: University of Chicago Press, 1966. The volume contains Leslie Fiedler's "The Blackness of Darkness: The Negro and the Development of American Gothic"; Marcus Klein's "Ralph Ellison's Invisible Man"; an interesting introduction by Gross, and several other helpful items.

Hill, Herbert, ed. *Anger and Beyond: The Negro Writer in the United States.* New York: Harper & Row, 1968. This volume contains essays by Jay Saunders Redding, LeRoi Jones, and Arna Bontemps, and a fine introduction by Hill.

Jones, LeRoi. "Myth of a Negro Literature," In *Home,* pp. 105–15. New York: William Morrow, 1966. This volume of Jones's essays also contains "LeRoi Jones Talking" and "The Revolutionary Theatre," two essays that have helped to point directions for present-day black writers.

Killens, John O. "The Black Writer vis-a-vis His Country." In *Black Man's Burden,* pp. 29–58. New York: Trident Press, 1965.

Littlejohn, David. *Black on White: A Critical Survey of Writing by American Negroes.* New York: Viking Press, 1969.

Margolies, Edward. *Native Sons: A Critical Study of Twentieth-Century Negro American Authors.* New York: J. B. Lippincott, 1969.

Mitchell, Lofton. *Black Drama: A History.* New York: Hawthorn Books, 1967.

Index

Abolitionist movement, 47, 50; as reflection of its age, 59–60; nature of, 59–60; newspapers of, 59; role of David Walker in, 66; role of Frederick Douglass in, 79–80
Abrahams, Roger, 37, 112
Adams, Henry, 47
Africa: culture, 43–44, folklore and literature, 14
African survivals, see Africa
Allen, W. F., 31
Antislavery movement, see Abolitionist movement
Arnold, Matthew, 9, 105–6; as a proponent of culture, 96–97
  Culture and Anarchy, 102

Baldwin, James, 40, 54–55, 81, 107–8, 120, 129; and apocalypse theme, 55
  "Alas, Poor Richard," 129
  The Fire Next Time, 40, 54–55
  Go Tell It on the Mountain, 40, 108, 81–83
  "Many Thousands Gone," 40
Barzun, Jacques, 5
Beauvoir, Simone de, 140
Beck, Robert
  Mama Black Widow, 115
  Pimp: The Story of My Life, 114
Bennett, Lerone, 59, 66
Bibb, Henry, 80
Black studies, in the American university, 118–21
Blauner, Robert, 110–11
Bontemps, Arna, 78, 107
  Black Thunder, 135
Brer Rabbit, 11, 24–27
Brewer, J. Mason, 11, 22
Brown, Claude, 39
Brown, H. Rap, 112, 117
Brown, John, 66; and Frederick Douglass, 81

Brown, Sterling, 20, 31, 127
Brown, William Wells, 59, 120
  Narrative of William Wells Brown, 80, 126

Carmichael, Stokeley, 112
Cassandra, John Anderson, 116
Caulfield, Mina Davis, 119
Césaire, Aimé, 14
Chesnutt, Charles, 38, 136
  The Conjure Woman, 38–39
Church, see Religion, black American
Civil War: black American view of, 50–51; effect on trickster hero, 24, 26
Clayton, Horace, 110
Cleaver, Eldridge, 81
  Soul on Ice, and David Walker's Appeal, 82–83
Collingwood, R. G., 142
Communist party, 125
Constitution (American), clauses insuring slavery, 3–4
Cowley, Malcolm, 125
Crisis, The, 107
Crossman, Richard, 128
Cruse, Harold, 17, 97
Cullen, Countee, 107
Culture
  African, 14, 43–44
  and critical standards, 6, 10
  as "a whole way of life," 1–2, 5–6
  as product of intellect and imagination, 16–17
  black American: and white culture theorizing, 11; cultural nationalism, 15–17; distinguishing traits, 16; study of, 142–44; history and, 2–4; of the ghetto, 109–21
  postindustrial Western conception of, 1, 5–6, 96–97
  theorizing on, 5–10

Culture (*cont.*)
  see also Du Bois, W. E. B., as black
    man of culture
Curry, Richard O., 60

Delaney, Martin, 135
Dobie, J. Frank, 29
Dorson, Richard, 20, 24, 29
Dos Passos, John, 125
Douglass, Frederick, 50, 79–83, 135
  "Fourth of July Oration," 50
  *Narrative of the Life of Frederick
    Douglass*, 50, 71–83; as *Bildungs-
    roman*, 76–77; as slave narrative,
    78–79; as black American auto-
    biography, 78–79; compared to
    David Walker's *Appeal*, 72
Drake, Sinclair, 110
Dreiser, Theodore, 125
Du Bois, W. E. B., 17, 32, 107–8, 130,
  136; and aestheticism, 96–97; and
  folk values, 105–7; and the "Talented
  Tenth," 98–99; as black man of cul-
  ture, 96–108; as model for black
  American authors, 107–8; attack on
  Booker T. Washington, 102–3; career
  of, 99–100; compared to Booker T.
  Washington, 103–5
  "A Litany at Atlanta," 99
  The Negro, 43
  The Philadelphia Negro, 109
  The Souls of Black Folk, 17; black
    man of culture in, 96–108
Dunbar, Paul Laurence, 38, 136
  "An Ante-Bellum Sermon," 13
  "We Wear the Mask," 14

Education, black American, 84–86; Da-
  vid Walker's view of, 84–85; Frederick
  Douglass's view of, 85; W. E. B. Du
  Bois's view of, 85; *see also* Douglass;
  Du Bois; Walker
Edwards, Jonathan, 42–43
Eliot, T. S., 18, 142
Elkins, Stanley, 143
Ellison, Ralph, 10, 35, 39, 40–41, 81,
  107–8, 120, 129, 132, 139
  Invisible Man, 10, 40–41, 108, 132;
    and Frederick Douglass's *Narra-
    tive*, 81–83
  Shadow and Act, 39
Emerson, Ralph Waldo, 89

Fisher, Rudolph, 107
Folk, black American: origin of, 19–20;
  unifying myth of, 44–46
Folklore, black American, 11–14, 18–41;
  and black American literature, 18–21;
  animal tales, 21–24; as indigenous expression of group, 118–19; badman
  hero, 36–38; ballads, 35–38; blues, 13,
  34–35; feat and contest heroes, 26–27;
  jubilee songs, 34; linguistic consid-
  erations, 119–20; lower-eschelon urban heroes, 36–38; preacher tales, 29;
  psychical aspect, 11–13, 22, 48–49,
  118–19; religious tales, 13, 28–29; testimonials, 13, 30–31; sermons, 13–14,
  29–30, 43, 52–53; spirituals, 12–13, 31–
  33, 43, 51, 53; subversive aspects, 11–
  12; supernatural tales, 27; trickster
  heroes, 11, 24–27; white America's
  conception of, 11, 134–35; work songs,
  33–34
Foner, Philip, 80
Franklin, Benjamin, 78, 89, 92
  Autobiography, 78, 118
Frazier, E. Franklin, 4, 43, 110

Garnet, Henry Highland, 59
Garrison, William Lloyd, 59
Ghetto, black American, 109–21; chang-
  ing concept of, 110–12; language of,
  112–15; study of language and cul-
  ture of, 115–21
Giovanni, Nikki, 118
Gloster, Hugh, 140
Gold, Mike, 127
Gordon, David, 44
Greenway, John, 43
Gullah Islands, 31, 47, 48, 113

Hammon, Jupiter, 69
Hampton Institute, 90
Harlan, Louis, 94
Harlem Renaissance, 39, 107
Harper, Frances E. W., 69
Harris, Joel Chandler, 11
  *Uncle Remus: His Songs and Say-
    ings*, 21
Henderson, Stephen, 124
Hernton, Calvin, 17
Herskovits, Melville J., 4, 43
Higginson, Thomas Wentworth, 31

Himes, Chester, 118
  If He Hollers, Let Him Go, 39
History, 2–4, 142–44
Horton, George Moses, 69
Howe, Irving, 136, 143
Howe, Julia Ward, 47
Hughes, Langston, 107, 125
  Not without Laughter, 118, 135
  Weary Blues, 14, 39–40
Hurston, Zora Neale, 30
  Jonah's Gourd Vine, 14, 52

Iceberg Slim, *see* Beck, Robert

Jackson, Andrew, 58
Jackson, Blyden, 122
Jasper, John, 43
  "De Sun Do Move," 30, 70
Jim Crow, legalization of, 86
Joans, Ted, 14
John cycle, *see* Folklore, black American, trickster heroes
"John Henry," *see* folklore, black American, ballads
John Reed Club, 125
Johnson, Charles S., 107
Johnson, James Weldon, 31, 41, 51, 136
  The Autobiography of an Ex-Colored Man, 135
  God's Trombones, 39, 107
Jones, Le Roi, 40, 54, 55–56; and apocalypse theme, 56
  Black Music, 40
  Blues People, 40
  "The Last Days of the American Empire," 55–56
Joyce, James, 142

Kelley, William Melvin, 17
Kennedy, John Pendleton, 12
King, Martin Luther, Jr., 81
Klapp, Orin, 27
Kochman, Thomas, 114
Krappe, Alexander Haggerty, 27
Krehbiel, Henry, 31

Language, *see* Ghetto, black American
Lawrence, D. H., 93–94
Lee, Don L., 14
Lewis, Oscar, 109
Lewis, R. W. B., 46

Literature, black American: and tradition, 18–21; apocalypse theme, 32, 42–57; autobiography, 78–79; difficulties of early authors, 135; early declamatory poets, 69; folklore as foundation, 14, 38–41; formalist poets, 79; oral tradition, 71; revolutionary stance, 56–57; slave narratives, 78, 80; theme of naming, 119–20
Little, Malcolm, *see* Malcolm X
Locke, Alain, 107
London, Jack, 47

McCall, Dan, 139
McKay, Claude, 39, 107
McKim, James, 33
M'Clellan, George, 79
Malcolm X, 120
  The Autobiography of Malcolm X, 14, 118
Marx, Leo, 46
Meier, August, 94
Migration, to the North, 109
Mill, John Stuart, 91
Miller, Perry, 46
Miscegenation, 132
Moynihan, Daniel Patrick, 110
Murphy, Jeanette Robinson, 44, 50
Music, *see* Folklore, black American
Myrdal, Gunnar, 94, 110
Myth, and black liberation, 44–46, 78–79

National Association for the Advancement of Colored People, 99–100, 128
Nationalism, *see* Culture, black American
Newman, John Henry, 116
Newspapers, 59
Newton, Huey P., 112
Niagara movement, 99–100
Northup, Solomon, 80

Pascal, Roy, 140
Pater, Walter, 96–97
Petry, Ann, 39
Phillips, U. B., 143
Plantation Tradition, 38
Plato, Ann, 79
Prosser, Gabriel, 103
Purvis, Robert, 59

Quarles, Benjamin, 59

Race, theorizing on, 5–6
Rainwater, Lee, 110
Randall, Dudley, 104–5
Ray, Henrietta Cordelia, 79
Redding, J. Saunders, 99n
Redmond, Charles, 59
Religion, black American: and Biblical history, 32; and Protestant tradition, 31, 43–44; and white religion, 45–46, 49; church of, 27–28, 84; eschatology and, 46; preacher and apocalypse theme, 51–53; *see also* Folklore, black American
Revolution, 56–57; *see also* Walker
Robinson, William, 69, 79

Sainte-Beuve, Charles, 18
Sartre, Jean Paul, 140
Scott, Nathan, 127
Seale, Bobby, 81
Segregation, *see* Jim Crow
Simonson, Harold, 46
Slave narratives, 78–79, 80
Slavery, 19–20
Smiles, Samuel, 89
Spirituals, 12–13, 31–33, 43, 51, 53
"Stackolee," 36–38
Stampp, Kenneth, 116
Steinbeck, John, 127
Stewart, William, 113
Stowe, Harriet Beecher, 47
Styron, William, 47

Thelwell, Mike, 14
Thurman, Wallace, 107
Toomer, Jean, 135
Tradition: literary, 18; sociohistorical, 18–21
Turner, Frederick Jackson, 46
Turner, Nat, 12, 103, 135
Tuskegee Institute, 90, 91–92, 93, 103

Vassa, Gustavus [Olaudah Equiano], 80
Vesey, Denmark, 12, 103

Walker, David, 49–50, 60–72, 83, 135
    Appeal; in Four Articles, 49–50, 60–72; apocalypse theme in, 62–64
Washington, Booker T., 50–51, 86–95; as agitator for black American liberty, 94–95; compared to W. E. B. Du Bois, 102–3
    Up From Slavery, 87–95
Webb, Constance, 129
West, Nathaniel, 47
Wheatley, Phillis, 79
Wilde, Oscar, 96–97
    Intentions, 97
Williams, John A., 143
Williams, Raymond, 5, 96
Wiltse, Charles, 66
Woodward, C. Vann, 86
Wright, Richard, 14, 20, 29, 107; and black American folk culture, 136–41; and existentialism, 140; life of, 122–31
    Black Boy, 39, 123, 128, 138–40
    Black Power, 130
    "Blueprint for Negro Literature," 141
    "Celebration," 131
    The Color Curtain, 130
    Eight Men, 129–30
    "Fire and Cloud," 126, 128
    "How 'Bigger' Was Born," 136–38
    "I Tried to Be a Communist," 128
    Lawd Today, 130
    The Long Dream, 130
    Native Son, 14, 39, 108, 126, 131–36, 140–41; and black American survival values, 135–36
    The Outsider, 129, 140
    Pagan Spain, 130
    Savage Holiday, 130
    Uncle Tom's Children, 126
    "The Voodoo of Hell's Half-Acre," 124